T0384431

Working Great!
Lean Leadership Lessons for Guiding Your Organization to Excellence

Working Great!
Lean Leadership Lessons for Guiding Your Organization to Excellence

Richard D. Brimeyer

Routledge
Taylor & Francis Group

A PRODUCTIVITY PRESS BOOK

Productivity Press
Taylor & Francis Group
6000 Broken Sound Parkway NW, Suite 300
Boca Raton, FL 33487-2742

© 2019 by Taylor & Francis Group, LLC
Productivity Press is an imprint of Taylor & Francis Group, an Informa business

No claim to original U.S. Government works

Printed on acid-free paper

International Standard Book Number-13: 978-1-138-48240-1 (Hardback)

Visit the Taylor & Francis Web site at
http://www.taylorandfrancis.com

and the CRC Press Web site at
http://www.crcpress.com

Contents

Preface

I owe most of my consulting success to my first employer, the predecessor companies of what is today called Danfoss Power Systems. Over the course of my 25-year career there, I received terrific training and incredible opportunities to put that training into practice.

I'd like to say that I was wise beyond my years in selecting the company as a 21-year-old college graduate, but that would be a stretch. The truth is, I was particularly swayed by a couple of individuals who I met during the interview process and by the fact that the company's headquarters was located in the same town (Ames, Iowa) as my alma mater (Iowa State University), which meant that I didn't have to relocate. So, in all truthfulness, inertia had more to do with my decision than keen foresight. Oh, and the fact that they made transmissions for fun vehicles like bulldozers, skid-steer loaders, combines, and street sweepers…the types of vehicles I pushed around in my sandbox as a young lad.

The company I joined in 1982 was very traditional in its management philosophies. Sure, working on various construction and farm equipment was a technical adventure for a young mechanical engineer, but the overall work environment was just so-so. I probably wouldn't have lasted ten years before moving on.

But then a truly wonderful thing happened that influenced my future satisfaction and success more than any technical challenges, formal training, or job opportunities. Something I could not have foreseen as I was vetting potential employers as a new graduate. Several years into my employment, a visionary leader named Dave took over the reins and transformed the company from a rigid hierarchical structure focused on pleasing bosses to an open, participatory, customer-focused organization.

The first two to three years of that transition were dedicated to changing the way everyone thought and acted—towards customers (external and internal), towards subordinates, and towards each other. We called them "soft skills."

Only then did we begin to dip our toes in the water by experimenting with various "hard skills" (what we today call Lean tools) such as creating flow cells, reducing changeover times, and batch sizes. During a recent discussion with Dave, I learned that the delayed introduction of tools was not so much a deliberate, brilliant strategy but rather the result of growing publicity and acceptance of Japanese manufacturing methods which weren't available at the beginning of the transformation. Basically, it was just dumb luck. Regardless, the atmosphere of trust and respect created during the prior years was necessary for smashing ancient paradigms of "the bigger the batch the better" and "workers are only capable of simple, highly specialized tasks."

Over the course of a decade, an exceptional organization transpired—an entrepreneurial Lean machine that served customers, owners, *and* employees equally well. While I'm sure that nostalgia somewhat taints my assessment, I'm confident that the vast majority of the 1000-plus employees who personally experienced the transformation still hold it as the benchmark for a workplace. The growth in revenues and earnings experienced during the same period serves as evidence that customers and owners made out okay too.

That experience shaped my philosophies as a Lean leader and later as a consultant. So, I will start with a simple conclusion: *Significant and sustained Lean success depends almost entirely on leaders and the culture they foster*. Sure, some area-specific, short-term gains can be realized via a top-down, tools-based approach. But broad, ongoing and organic improvement that is embraced by almost all employees requires a unique environment, one carefully defined and nurtured by leaders.

Unfortunately, many (perhaps most) leaders embark on their Lean initiative with a focus on tools either observed during a benchmarking tour, disclosed during a short symposium presentation, or peddled by their chosen Lean partner... often an almost equally inexperienced "expert" from the local community college or a practitioner recently laid off and now "consulting." These leaders are thus ill-equipped to understand the critical behavior and attitude changes required of them and their staff in order to sustain tools-based improvements and, more importantly, to effectively promote and harvest their employees' innovation to remove waste.

Working Great! is my attempt to share the most important lessons learned while leading within the transformation described above and guiding several other organizations through their own makeovers as a consultant. Unlike travel brochures and websites created by a tour company or the local visitors' bureau for the sole purpose of promoting a highly predictable vacation trip, *Working Great!* strives to provide an honest, clear, culture-first handbook of leadership skills and techniques (with some tools) required to effectively guide one's organization through a Lean expedition.

Intentionally unsophisticated, *Working Great!* avoids the use of most Japanese Lean terms for a couple of reasons. I cut my Lean teeth in a UAW facility where one could get beat up simply for saying "poka yoke." Out of self-preservation, I avoided such terms. More importantly, the Japanese terms tend to add an unnecessary element of mystery to what should be primarily common sense.

In fact, I would argue that when we speak of a healthy Lean culture the term "Lean" itself is redundant. The many positive aspects of such a culture are desired within any great working environment. The leadership behaviors for promoting such a culture are therefore consistent not only with Lean leadership, but with good leadership.

Thus, *Working Great!* is intended for a broad range of leader-managers including:

- Leaders considering whether to embark on a Lean initiative within their organization or who are just getting started on one.
- Managers and supervisors striving to understand their changing roles in a Lean environment.
- Newly appointed supervisors wanting to hit the ground running (regardless of whether in a Lean organization or not).
- Managers and supervisors struggling with employee interactions and striving to improve (regardless of whether in a Lean organization or not).

But most of all, *Working Great!* is intended for those not content to simply consume information, but rather those with the curiosity and courage to try applying newfound knowledge. When leading people, it's not what we know that matters but rather what we do with what we know.

As such, this book is not written to be a page-turner that entices the reader to go cover-to-cover uninterrupted. Rather, the format is one of distinct but interconnected lessons, with the intent that each be consumed, contemplated, and put to use. To support that approach each lesson is accompanied with suggested application challenges.

It is my hope that *Working Great!* will be a worthy text for leadership book clubs with participants sharing their experiences and encouraging each other to apply the various lessons.

The weekly pace suggested by the lesson headings may make sense from the standpoint of a weekly point of focus for improvement-minded managers. The weekly cadence, however, is obviously not realistic in terms of representing an actual Lean expedition. Perhaps the most appropriate pace is one that allows the desired behavior(s) of each individual lesson to become a habit which behavioral scientists tell us takes several weeks.

Finally, a word of encouragement: Everything appears pretty straightforward while reading from the serenity of one's favorite nook. There are a lot more moving parts when applying lessons with real people at work amid the fog of war. The interaction or implementation that goes as smoothly as envisioned during reading is rare indeed.

But take heart. The good news is that employees recognize your efforts if you are persistent and your intent is noble. With continued practice the game slows down. At that point you realize that, amid all the noise, all you are trying to do is to create a place where employees are challenged and allowed to grow while providing great products/services to customers. When you create such a place, all other career achievements pale in comparison.

Best wishes for a rewarding expedition!

Acknowledgments

A quick shout-out to all those who intentionally taught, mentored, and nurtured me, starting with Mom and Dad and continuing with a long line of dedicated instructors throughout my formal education at St. Anthony's Elementary School, Wahlert High School, Loras College, and Iowa State University.

Thanks to all my past supervisors at Danfoss Power Solutions and Lean Partners for providing meaningful work, great training, and examples of (mostly) great leadership.

Special thanks to all the people I supervised who were patient with my mistakes and cared enough to provide feedback when I screwed up.

Hats off to a wonderful group of clients referenced throughout this work who are committed to creating a Lean culture and make work fun. I especially appreciate your willingness to open your doors and share your successes with others.

My sincere gratitude goes to Productivity Press for taking a chance on a new author, specifically Meredith Norwich and Michael Sinocchi for guiding me through the process.

Finally and foremost, thanks to Janet for being the best roommate, friend, and business partner that anyone could ask for over the past 35 years. In hindsight, I was remiss when I excluded proofreading in our vows, but I was afraid you might bail.

Chapter 1

January—Preparing for an Expedition: Assessing the Resolve and Resources to Succeed

One of the most fascinating books I've listened to is the audio version of Candice Millard's *The River of Doubt*. Millard chronicles the exploration of an unmapped Brazilian tributary to the Amazon in 1913–1914 by a party led by Theodore Roosevelt and Cândido Rondon. Millard provides an incredibly in-depth look into the adventure, including the planning stage. Here, questionable motivations by key participants, miscalculations, and poor assumptions made months prior to embarking proved fateful for some members and almost doomed the entire party.[1]

The common term "journey" seems a bit too tame to characterize a Lean initiative or any cultural change for that matter. The undertaking is simply fraught with too many potential pitfalls to imply that the desired destination—if it is even known—is a given. Like Roosevelt's adventure, "expedition" seems much more appropriate.

While thoughtful planning cannot guarantee success, poor planning certainly assures failure. Two ingredients stand out as absolutely necessary:

1. A properly motivated and committed leader is foremost. Untold setbacks will require inexhaustible encouragement and sharing of the vision. If personal gain is the leader's motivation, those inspirations will surely ring hollow.
2. Access to an experienced guide is critical. Beware of anyone who claims to have made the trip before and knows the way. Your expedition will be different.

1

Rather, the right guide knows the territory and possesses the skills and adaptability to survive within that territory. Rondon's years of experience in the Amazon jungle proved absolutely essential to survival on the River of Doubt.

Before embarking on your expedition, make absolutely sure you know why it is necessary and identify who you will trust to guide you along the way.

Week 1 – Real Improvement Requires Real Change

'Tis the season for making personal resolutions. According to a poll conducted by CBS in 2013, roughly a third of us make an improvement promise to ourselves at the beginning of the new year.[2] Most involve health (lose weight, quit smoking, drink less) while others strive to improve a relationship, find a better job, further education, or save more money.

Unfortunately, the enthusiasm doesn't last long. Researchers at Scranton University reported that almost a quarter of well-intenders fall off the wagon during the first week and roughly half during the first month.[3] The defection rate slows considerably after that, reinforcing the theory that it takes several weeks to change a habit.

Forty percent claim to be still working on their resolution after six months. Ultimately, less than ten percent of resolution goals are achieved.

And that's just one person trying to change! Is it any wonder then that leading change within an organization is *really* tough?

Every couple of months I receive a call from an organization inquiring about my services. Occasionally the caller is the senior leader, in which case I get pretty excited. But too often the call is delegated, as if leading an organization through change is akin to changing the oil in the company's vehicles.

The calls often go something like this:

Caller: We're interested in eliminating the waste in our (fill in the blank) process. Our president recently attended a seminar on Lean and she's convinced that this can really help us.

Rick: I see. So tell me, how do your employees feel? Do they recognize problems with the process?

Caller: Oh no. They're pretty comfortable with the way things are. In fact, it will be a battle to get them to change.

Rick: Well, I can certainly help you improve your process. But if you want those changes to stick, we're going to have to change the way your employees think. We'll have to make them sensitive to problems and motivated to solve them. That involves a lot more effort than a three-day process improvement event and it involves your management team.

Caller: Oh…okay, we'll get back to you.

Needless to say, few call back.

Those that stick with the conversation know there isn't a silver bullet tool that will solve their situation any more than the latest fad diet will help them keep 30 pounds off forever.

Improved results come from changed behaviors. Changing organizational results means changing the behaviors of the majority of people within the organization. In order to do that, the habits and ultimately the core beliefs of the organization must change. That's not something achieved over a couple of weeks.

Obviously, while knowledge of various tools and techniques is necessary for successful implementation, sustained success goes way beyond education. If education was enough to drive change, there wouldn't be a smoker left in the country. Yet, time and again, we see increases in cigarette taxes more effective than any new warning or TV commercial citing the dangers of smoking.

Unfortunately, a lot of dollars are foolishly spent each year providing cursory training, thinking that employees will emerge from a two-hour introductory class as born-again waste avengers. I suspect that's often the next call made following the aborted conversation above.

So, if you're still game for implementing real, lasting, and positive change within your organization, here are some thoughts for getting started:

- Clearly articulate why change is needed. You're likely battling complacency, especially in a strengthening economy. Don't keep your concerns to yourself.
- Identify the core beliefs that drive behaviors today and what those beliefs must become.
- Specify behaviors of managers and supervisors that reinforce the old belief system and required changes to support the new belief system. Creating management behavior lists to start doing, stop doing, do more of, and do less of can be very helpful.
- Make it clear that this is where you are going. Patience is required, especially with those making a real effort to change. Realize, however, that ultimately success will depend on the actions of managers and supervisors. Hold them accountable.

The good news is that some people do successfully realize New Year's resolutions. Some leaders do lead their organizations to dramatically higher levels of performance. Granted, it's a small percentage of those that try. But for those that succeed, it's life-changing.

Application Challenges

- Give careful thought to the questions of the top three bullets above for your organization.

- Ask a couple of trusted and respected peers or staff members that know your organization well to complete the same exercise for your organization. Are you confident in your assessment?
- Understand that improving an organization is the most challenging—and rewarding—effort that a leader can undertake. It is an ultramarathon requiring perseverance, courage, discipline, and more personal commitment than one can imagine standing at the starting line. Imagine and quantify the potential benefits. Are you up for the expedition? Read on...

Week 2 – Keys to Lean Success

As a consultant specializing in Lean methodologies, I'm occasionally asked to identify the primary factors in determining an organization's degree of successful implementation. My list is surprisingly short.

The first factor is typically evident by the time we complete our first phone conversation. In fact, I generally have a decent read as soon as I understand who I'm talking to and where they fit within the potential client's organization. Factor number one is simply the commitment level of the senior leader.

So, when Fort Dodge City Manager David Fierke personally contacted me in early 2009 and clearly articulated his vision for how Lean methods could help his organization, the first hurdle to success was practically cleared. Today, other municipalities are calling David and his leadership team asking for advice.

Likewise, when I received an impassioned plea for help in late 2011 from Nicole Vivacqua of Fairfield Line, a multigeneration family business facing some stiff challenges, one of my first questions regarded the caller's position within the company. No doubt my pulse quickened when she responded, "It's my business!"

Obviously, the phone call itself is not paramount. But investing the personal time to investigate and phone screen potential consultants is indicative of the level of ownership which the senior leader personally feels to the success of the effort.

During the course of the call we discuss how success will ultimately be determined by the culture of the organization, that is, the mindset of the employees. We discuss how changing organizational culture always lies with leadership.

At this point in the conversation I ask if the leader is prepared to make the tough decisions, to the point of slaying some sacred cows if necessary.

"We have to!" was David's response. "We have no other choice."
"Absolutely!" was Nicole's answer. Her voice was as convincing as her choice of words.

Factor number two is a strong offshoot of factor number one. It is the quality and availability of the internal resource assigned to become the internal coordinator for the initiative. While the senior leader is ultimately responsible for establishing the environment where the effort can be successful, it typically isn't realistic for them to also become the technical expert on the various tools.

Let's be honest; some consultants overstay their welcome. Occasionally that's because the organization hasn't done an adequate job of weaning itself. Selecting a capable and available internal expert therefore guards against that occurrence.

Thus, selecting a very capable employee to be a liaison to the external consultant is critical. This individual is responsible for absorbing as much knowledge and experience from the consultant as possible and for helping the organization to effectively apply it. The ideal internal candidate should be a quick learner and be respected by others within the organization as a high performer.

The selection of the internal resource and the amount of time they're expected to support the effort is the ultimate reflection of the senior leader's commitment. In the case of the City of Fort Dodge, David tapped one of his most trusted staff members and made the Lean transformation his top priority. At Fairfield Line, Nicole selected an up-and-comer with a passion for Lean and learning, and also made it his top priority.

I strongly suspect that these two factors accurately predict success not only with a Lean initiative, but with any organizational change that ultimately relies on new behaviors and new ways of thinking. In such cases, the senior leader should have their hands securely on the wheel.

Application Challenges

- Any organizational change effort can only succeed to the level of the highest committed leader, assuming that leader's leader is at least supportive. Clearly define your sphere of influence in the organization within which you will impact change.
- Build your case for change and ensure that your leader is supportive.
- Identify potential candidates for an internal expert. If no strong internal candidates exist, one will have to be developed or hired.

Week 3 – Benefiting from Fresh Eyes

Over the course of my career I've made a somewhat sad, but certainly not surprising observation: those most adamant that there is nothing to be gained from an outside opinion are typically the people who need it the most.

Recently I was facilitating a process improvement event. One of the participants had obviously been "strongly encouraged" to attend. He stewed in his seat with his arms tightly crossed. He proudly proclaimed during introductions that he had been performing the task under review for 25 years and he saw no value in wasting time on an already-optimized process.

I quickly glanced at my watch. "Only 20 minutes into day one; that's a new personal record for initial verbal resistance," I marveled to myself. "There's likely to be more opportunity here than I initially thought."

I assured Mr. Adamant that his feelings were not uncommon and asked him to trust the improvement process that we were about to embark upon, explaining that it had proven itself effective time and time again.

Sure enough, less than two hours later (another personal record), the team had identified a major process improvement and was in the process of implementing its breakthrough. Over the course of the next three days, several other improvements would be identified, tested, modified, implemented, and finally documented into standard work.

To his credit, at the end of the three days Mr. Adamant shook my hand and thanked me for the help.

As a former general manager used to regularly remind me and my colleagues on his staff, "We don't know what we don't know." This was his way of encouraging us to continually explore outside of our comfort zone.

Indeed, savvy leaders understand this and make conscious efforts to introduce themselves to new people, fresh situations, and innovative ideas that help them illuminate their organization's blind spots.

There are many ways to go about obtaining these "fresh eyes."

Perhaps the most important is to ensure that the senior management staff doesn't become overweighted with members that have grown up in the organization. While it's nice to promote from within, it's critical that top management contain a balance of capable members with a different set of experiences. The current and desired ratio of company veterans to newcomers should be considered whenever filling a management opening.

For smaller organizations, or those that do not frequently experience management turnover, a trusted consultant or advisor can provide an invaluable perspective. A consultant's constant exposure to other organizations, not to mention industries, as well as their ability rise to above the trees and assess the forest can complement your detailed understanding of your business.

Benchmarking is another means for obtaining an outsider's perspective. This is most valuable when a specific weakness is identified, and an organization is visited which excels in the targeted weakness. A game plan for the visit should be predetermined with expectations that those visiting will be accountable for identifying and implementing an improvement plan.

Reciprocal tours with area businesses can also be helpful. In order to be truly meaningful, ground rules should be established which makes it not only acceptable but expected that participants provide tour hosts with insightful, honest, and critical feedback rather than "happy talk."

Finally, any method of learning broadens an understanding of the organization. Formal classes, books, magazine articles, seminars, webinars…the list goes on and on.

What we're talking about with any of the above strategies is a means for nurturing a learning organization; one which welcomes rather than resists new ideas and opportunities.

Application Challenges

- Brainstorm various means to gain a "fresh eyes" perspective.
- Set a personal goal for the year for a set number of experiences, taking advantage of several different ideas from your list. Monitor progress!
- Repeat the above exercise with your direct reports. Monitor progress!

Week 4 – Choosing a Guide for the Expedition

During the throes of the Great Recession, Bill Gross, Mohamed El-Erian, and some smart folks at PIMCO developed a theory that it was unreasonable to expect nominal (including inflation) GDP to continue at the 6–7 percent annual rate that existed for the past 20–25 years heading into the crisis. Basically, the thought was that governments would reign in capitalism by promoting reduced borrowing, reduced globalization, and increased regulation. Termed "The New Normal," Gross and El-Erian predicted future nominal GDP growth at roughly half the recent historical trend.[4]

Like most economic theories, The New Normal opened the doors for intense debate. Its authors may have been a bit pessimistic—the post-Recession GDP has run closer to 60 percent of its pre-Recession value—likely goosed by unprecedented and unforeseen quantitative policies by central banks.[5]

There's little debate, however, that we have and likely will continue to experience significantly slower growth than that experienced through the 1980s, 1990s, and early 2000s. Your organization can no longer simply rely on a rising tide to lift all boats. In order to thrive, fundamental changes will be required to distinguish your organization from its competitors. This means significantly better products or services and/or vastly superior performance in delivering those products and services (e.g., faster response, higher quality, lower cost).

By its very definition, *fundamental* change implies that it is outside of your organization's historical competency. We're talking about changing not only how people perform their jobs, but more importantly, how they think about them. This typically requires the help of an outside resource. Several factors should be considered when choosing a guide for your Lean expedition.

First, understand that the number of people calling themselves consultants increases with the unemployment rate. This is a frequent first-stop for professionals with ten or more years of experience who just received a pink slip. As the unemployment rate falls, the majority return to traditional jobs. Thus, a logical first sort is to select those that have been in business through an entire economic cycle.

Second, keep in mind the warning of American psychologist Abraham Maslow who reminded us that if the only tool you have is a hammer, there is a tendency to treat everything as if it were a nail. Many consultants will attempt to sell you a *tool*...the use of which they coincidentally are an expert.

Rather, the top consideration should be to identify someone that has demonstrated expertise in establishing a Lean *culture*. Sustained improvement requires positive changes in employees' mindsets; they must embrace continued use of the new Lean tools long after the consultant is gone.

This is only accomplished by actively involving employees in the change process. The consultant must therefore be an expert on the process for leading change within an organization. The right candidate must not only earn your trust, but also must be capable of winning the trust of your employees.

If your organization involves manufacturing, prospects should have demonstrated successes in both the factory and office support functions. The best way to verify demonstrated successes is via references. Any reputable consulting organization should have multiple clients willing to sing their praises. In addition to talking to the leaders of these happy customers, visit their facilities so you can see and hear about their experiences firsthand from employees. Provided you're not a direct competitor, most organizations are happy to share their successes.

By now it should be clear that the right consultant for your organization may very well not be the lowest cost provider. The goal is not to realize the smallest outlay, but rather the largest return. When we selected a surgeon for our daughter the first question was, "How often have you successfully completed this procedure?" The same question is valid when choosing the right person to operate on your organization.

Application Challenges

- Clearly articulate the desired outputs of the change and why these are important.
- Work with a financial expert to estimate the relative scale of the payback if successful.
- Brainstorm various sources for locating a guide.
- Work with a couple of trusted and respected peers or staff members that know your organization well to complete the selection criteria and begin interviewing.

References

1. Millard, Candice. 2005. *The River of Doubt: Theodore Roosevelt's Darkest Journey.* New York: The Doubleday Broadway Publishing Group.

2. CBS New York. 2013. Poll: Most Americans don't make New Year's resolutions, go out to celebrate. http://newyork.cbslocal.com/2013/12/29/poll-most-americans-dont -make-new-years-resolutions-go-out-to-celebrate/ (accessed Oct. 5, 2017).
3. Flatow, Ira and Dr. John Norcross. NPR. *Talk of the Nation, Science Friday*. Dec. 26, 2008. http://www.npr.org/templates/story/story.php?storyId=98738130 (accessed Oct. 5, 2017).
4. Gross, W.H. PIMCO. *Economic Outlook*. October 2009. Mohamed El-Erian and Bill Gross discuss PIMCO's cyclical outlook and the New Normal. http://europe.pimco .com/EN/Insights/Pages/New%20Normal%20QA%20Gross%20El-Erian%20 Oct%202009.aspx (accessed Oct. 5, 2017).
5. Amadeo, Kimberly. The Balance. U.S. GDP by year compared to recessions and events: The strange ups and downs of the U.S. economy since 1929. Updated Sept. 6, 2017. https://www.thebalance.com/us-gdp-by-year-3305543 (accessed Oct. 5, 2017).

Chapter 2

February—Defining the Wilderness: Creating the Place for Lean to Succeed

Many managers and supervisors are chosen for their role because of a demonstrated ability to get things done. They're a closer.

While no doubt an admirable trait, a successful Lean expedition is definitely not a race. Rather than checking off benchmarks (or tools) attained on a to-do list, the emphasis must be on creating a place where common beliefs are shared and demonstrated, initially by leaders and eventually by almost all employees.

As a recovering engineer, this was a revelation. Nothing in my formal education dealt with the intangible, but very real, success factors of emotional intelligence, engagement, and culture. In fact, I managed engineers and production employees for almost 20 years before I realized that my first priority was not designing and building great *products*...rather it was *developing great people* that could be successful designing and building great products!

I've heard stories of sensei from Toyota that insist clients master 5S for two years prior to moving on to more advanced tools. Their reasoning is that the visual nature of 5S makes it obvious whether the generic improvement process of identifying an improvement, standardizing the improvement, and following the new standard is hardwired into the organization. If not, expecting sustained success with less visual tools and improvements is futile. In other words, how can we expect employees to respect a relatively invisible standard such as lubricating a machine at a prescribed frequency if they disregard a very visual standard such as where a particular wrench is stored?

In essence, they are ensuring a culture of Plan–Do–Check–Act (PDCA) discipline is in place. While certainly important, the following beliefs are equally valuable:

■ Our work is meaningful; we have customers who are real people with (mostly) reasonable expectations and our livelihood depends on our ability to consistently meet, even exceed, those expectations.
■ Work is made up of processes which can always be improved; waste is the enemy of all.
■ Unleashing employee creativity is paramount to eliminating waste; it requires mutual trust and respect.

If an organization spends two years to embed such a belief system prior to introducing a single tool, it will be time well spent.

Week 5 – Taking the Mystery Out of Culture

Regardless of the type of work your organization performs, there are three generic ingredients required for success:

1. Quality tools and processes
2. A knowledgeable and skilled workforce
3. A healthy mindset throughout the organization

Whether your organization builds homes or educates students, is public or private, employs one or hundreds, neglecting just one of these key elements is potentially lethal.

Let's take the example of a restaurant. What's required to coax patrons back time and time again when so many choices are available to them?

1. The right cooking equipment, quality ingredients, and great recipes
2. Chefs and waitstaff competent in consistently turning orders into delicious meals
3. Staff that always portray that they thoroughly enjoy taking care of customers

The third ingredient, often referred to as the culture of the organization, is the most difficult to assess and perfect. Culture can be defined as the shared, learned, and implied values, beliefs, and attitudes that shape and influence a group's perceptions and behaviors. Think of culture as the collective emotional environment of the organization.

Unfortunately, many leaders mistakenly either dismiss culture as irrelevant or shrouded in mystery and beyond their ability to impact, akin to an adolescent's mood swings. They incorrectly conclude that the business gods indiscriminately bestow great cultures on a few chosen organizations, just as a few individuals are blessed with high intelligence, great public speaking skills, and other desirable attributes.

But wait! We now know that with focused attention, time, and (in some cases) a little money, individuals can positively impact many of the personal traits that prior generations thought of as intrinsic. The same goes for an organization's culture. Granted, defining and influencing the attributes of a group are much more difficult because complexity increases with each additional person.

Assessing and positively impacting the culture of an organization is the unique responsibility of leadership.

It starts by gleaning brutally honest observations from a cross-section of individuals who see your organization from differing viewpoints (employees, customers, and vendors) to identify its current norms. How do we *really* behave? What do our actions reveal about what's *really* important to us (regardless of what's posted on the walls)?

Once the current true culture is understood, an inventory of strengths and weaknesses is created. The gap between the current reality and the future goal is defined with potentially lethal flaws prioritized as initial targets.

Once again, the work of eliminating cultural weaknesses falls distinctly on leadership, beginning at the very top. Long-lasting successful change depends more on how leaders are observed to behave rather than anything we say or write. In short, it's imperative that leaders consistently model the very behaviors that we desire from employees in the new culture.

Let's say an organization determines that its members hoard valuable information in an effort to increase their perceived importance and job security. Leadership might define their specific actions as follows:

- Increase transparency by sharing pertinent business information each quarter in all-employee talks delivered as a leadership team
- Start evaluating employees for teamwork when making promotions and annual evaluations
- Avoid hiring "lone rangers" regardless of their work experience and skills
- Boost recognition of team accomplishments and de-emphasize individual deeds
- Implement a formal mentoring program
- Ensure that managers are visibly working on projects together

It's often helpful when identifying these leadership behaviors to think in terms of what do we need to start doing? Stop doing? Do more of? Do less of?

Modifying an organization's culture is a slow, tedious process to be sure. Positive change will only occur after months of concerted effort. Rest assured, however, that real change is indeed possible and worth the time. Unlike the first two ingredients listed above, a first-class culture is an almost invisible competitive advantage.

Application Challenges

- Ask trusted customers, vendors, and employees that know your organization well to identify its current norms. How do we *really* behave? What do our actions reveal about what's *really* important to us?
- Identify the desired norms and beliefs.
- For each discrepancy, identify the management behaviors to start doing, stop doing, do more of and do less of to promote the new norms.
- Read *Leading Change* by John P. Kotter; it's a logical and surprisingly straightforward masterpiece on a complex subject.[1]

Week 6 – Maslow and Motivation

In the early twentieth century, psychological research focused on extreme deviants in an attempt to identify the cause(s) of their conditions. That changed with Abraham Maslow, who opted instead to focus on successful outliers, such as Albert Einstein and Eleanor Roosevelt, to determine what distinguished them. The findings in his 1943 paper entitled "A Theory of Human Motivation" contain precious secrets for anyone who manages people.[2]

Maslow defined what he called a hierarchy of needs which is often pictorially depicted as a pyramid (Figure 2.1). The foundation of the pyramid includes basic, physiological needs such as food, water, clothing, shelter, and rest.

The next higher level is safety and security. These include such requirements as physical and emotional safety, steady employment, and financial security.

The third level of needs is love and belonging. Examples include acceptance, being part of a family, and teamwork.

Maslow's fourth level identified our need for self-esteem. It includes a sense of accomplishment, recognition, respect, and self-confidence.

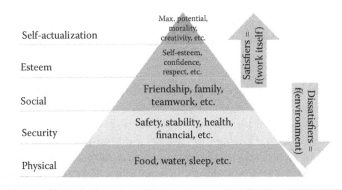

Figure 2.1 Maslow's hierarchy of needs.

Finally, at the peak of Maslow's pyramid is self-actualization. This includes realizing a high sense of purpose and the ability to creatively use one's unique skills and talents to make the world a slightly better place.

So what does all this have to do with managing people? First of all, employees' physical and security needs must be met. This includes:

■ Pay must allow employees to meet basic needs, provide for some future security, and be perceived as fair.
■ The physical working environment must be safe and reasonably comfortable.
■ Employees need to feel emotionally safe at work.

Each employee has their own minimum acceptable levels for these factors. Not meeting those minimum standards results in demotivation. According to research by Gallup, 18 percent of all North American employees (24 percent worldwide) are actively disengaged…they hate their job.[3]

Interestingly, research by Frederick Herzberg concluded that one can't effectively motivate employees via the bottom two levels.[4] We can only demotivate by not meeting minimum requirements. Exceeding those requirements doesn't enhance motivation.

For example, consider those who follow the oil boom to North Dakota. They endure dangerous conditions under extreme weather, often without family. They are handsomely compensated, but are they truly motivated? Bribed might be a better description. Many have plans to simply endure for a while, make a quick buck and move on to other opportunities which fulfill higher level needs on Maslow's pyramid.

True motivation occurs by developing an environment where the higher-level needs of belonging, self-esteem, and self-actualization are regularly attained. Examples include:

■ A team environment exists where work is fairly shared and workers appreciate each other as individuals.
■ Employees are trusted to make appropriate decisions, recognized for their contributions, and never taken for granted.
■ The work is meaningful and challenging, often requiring employees to learn new skills.

Again, as an example, consider that some of the most engaged workers on the planet are employed by nonprofits. Their pay is likely on the lower side, but it is adequate and fair. What sets them apart is that they are surrounded by a team that, like them, is committed to a cause.

Situated between demotivated and motivated employees are those who are neither. Their physiological and security needs are met, but their social, esteem, and self-actualization needs go unfulfilled. To them, it's basically "a job." They will do what it takes to remain on the payroll, but little more. Although they may not actively seek out other employment opportunities, they are willing to listen when a headhunter calls. Gallup's research indicates that 54 percent of North American employees (63 percent worldwide) fit in this category.[3]

This is impactful stuff! Motivated and engaged employees accomplish much more than unengaged employees. They go the extra mile to keep customers happy, identify problems before they become a crisis, and care enough to make improvements. Best of all, motivated employees typically aren't even interested in listening to external opportunities.

The bottom two tiers of Maslow's pyramid can generally be accomplished with tolerable management and adequate funding for compensation, physical workspace, and safety resources. The top three tiers simply cannot be purchased. They require leaders that understand what really makes people tick and are willing to invest personally in creating such a place. Recall that the top three tiers are what fuels motivation and engagement. Perhaps that's why Gallup's research indicates that less than one in three North American employees (13 percent worldwide) is truly engaged.[3]

Application Challenges

- Grade your organization for each level of Maslow's pyramid.
- If your scores on the bottom two layers (basic physical and security) are low, address these before proceeding.
- Set a goal for one social activity per month for your team. Perhaps you'll have lunch together and not talk about work, take a walk around the building, or initiate a service project. Challenge a different team member to organize each month's activity.
- Set a goal to recognize a team member each week. Be timely, specific, and (most importantly) genuine in your praise.

Week 7 – Employees That Give a Rip

During a four-week span in late 2009 I had discussions with four different business leaders who each identified a need to fine-tune the customer attentiveness of their employees. I didn't give much thought to the initial report, but as I heard the same message repeated multiple times in close succession, my ears perked up and I started to delve deeper.

These leaders felt like their organizations were decent, perhaps even good at serving customers. What gnawed at them was that they realized they weren't great. The gap in performance perhaps wasn't critically apparent when business was booming but increased competition during the prolonged recession clearly brought it to light.

Furthermore, they acknowledged that competition was likely to remain fierce going forward. Now that they were emerging from survival mode and beginning to think once again about playing offense, they saw this as an area of strategic need.

Providing *personalized* service is the cornerstone to any successful business relationship. Obviously, the product or service provided has to be of high quality at a good value or the customer will go elsewhere. But what turns *satisfied* customers into *loyal* customers is how they are served and how that service makes them feel.

Four tactics are especially effective when providing personalized service:

1. Use *names*, both yours and theirs: No one wants to be treated like a number (unless perhaps it's number one). Even if the customer doesn't volunteer their name, we can generally learn it during the interaction and should use it.
2. Exhibit *empathy*: Not everyone thinks and behaves like we do. Employees should be trained to recognize customers' potential desires, fears, and concerns and know how to respond to them. Effectively learning to do this expands our market to the majority of the world that doesn't share our background or point of view.
3. Make effective use of *space*: Break down both literal and figurative barriers that separate us from customers. Like empathy, this takes skill to distinguish what's appropriate for each customer since each will be different. Greeting the customer in their space with a firm, friendly handshake is generally a good place to start.
4. Make the experience *special*: Let the customer know that serving them is a joy and not a chore. I recently watched a teller in an adjoining lane at my bank help a customer resolve an issue over the phone. She was smiling and even shared a friendly laugh as she worked through the problem. I don't know if the root error was caused by the bank or the customer but regardless, I'm confident that customer will be retained due to the service received.

So how do we best ensure that employees learn and practice these skills? Training certainly helps (and you can rest assured that, after hearing of the need four times in a month, I fine-tuned my materials). But remember—training is best utilized for addressing deficiencies in skills rather than shortcomings in motivation.

In order to provide the necessary motivation and to reinforce classroom lessons, employees need to see their managers modeling the desired behaviors, providing personalized service not only to customers but also to employees. That's right; we can't expect employees to treat customers any better than they're being treated themselves.

1. Are you referring to your employees by the name they desire to be called?
2. Do you understand their dreams? Their fears? Their joys and pressures away from work?

3. Do you meet them where they work or do they always have to come to your office to talk?
4. Finally, do they know that you appreciate them?

If the answer to any of the above is not an unqualified "Yes!" you've got an area for improvement. By successfully addressing it, you should begin to observe employees taking better care of coworkers and customers.

Application Challenges

- Create a "database" of information on your employees. What are the names of their significant others and children? What are their hobbies? Pet Peeves? Aspirations? (This information will be extremely useful when we start rounding.)
- Identify at least one or two unique skills or traits that you appreciate in each employee; something that you can *genuinely* recognize them for.

Week 8 – Making Work Meaningful

Back when I engineered transmissions for road construction equipment, I loved to observe our customers' products at work in the field. My family accused me of planning our vacations *for* road construction. As other stalled drivers were throwing up their hands while waiting in line behind the flag person, I was as happy as a kid at an amusement park.

Thus, it was particularly eye opening when I was assigned to a facility in Illinois which manufactured components for those same transmissions. Here, employees were roughly 300 miles away from their transmission assembly line customers. More importantly, they were one link further removed from the end customer in the supply chain. Most had no idea where their handiwork eventually ended up.

This situation was epitomized for me during an open house tour when I observed one of our machinists point to a machined casting and explain to his family, "That's my hole." From that point it became my personal mission to increase the meaning in our employees' work.

We started by taking a group of supervisors and employees to tour the assembly plant each month. Here, they got to see their components being assembled, meet their immediate customers, and discuss issues face-to-face. Suddenly, "those idiots in Iowa" became reasonable folks.

The highlight of the day was buckling them into the seat of a skid steer loader or a bulldozer and watching looks of sheer terror turn into excitement as they gained confidence in controlling the vehicle. The trips were talked about for months afterwards.

I encouraged our sales folks to help themselves to every brochure in our customers' literature racks for vehicles which used our products and asked them to send them to our facility. I would translate the product used into the components which our employees produced and thus post the pamphlets on the appropriate cell's bulletin board.

We had our field service team visit the plant to provide lessons on how the product worked and which of the many features we machined were most important to the performance and life of the vehicle it would ultimately propel.

In short, our employees no longer simply drilled holes into chunks of cast iron. They became responsible for entire components, knew the names of the people in Iowa that assembled them, what features were most important and why, and that they eventually ended up in a Caterpillar road roller, Bobcat skid steer loader, or some other specific piece of equipment. (Perhaps they even started to plan their vacations for road construction.)

Patrick Lencioni's book *The Truth About Employee Engagement* (recommended reading for anyone supervising people) highlights three ingredients for unfulfilling work:

1. Anonymity (i.e., "I don't matter.")
2. Irrelevance (i.e., "My work doesn't matter.")
3. Lack of measurement (i.e., "My performance doesn't matter.")[5]

Any of Lencioni's three signs result in a serious deficiency of the Meaning Quotient or "MQ" of work, a term coined in a January 2013 *McKinsey Quarterly* article.[6]

Since the mid-1990s, John Deere's Gold Key program has allowed customers to tour final assembly plants to observe vehicles being built, even starting up their vehicle with the signature gold key at the completion of the tour.[7] Deere's Waterloo plant alone hosts over 3000 such tours annually.[8] That's an average of over 12 per workday!

While Deere no doubt gains customer loyalty points through the Gold Key program, the biggest benefit may very well be the personal significance and sense of accomplishment which each of the assembly workers receives as they complete their portion of work under the watchful eyes of expectant customers, many who have traveled for several hours to observe the process.

The next time you find yourself lamenting that "nobody cares," take a good look in the mirror. And get to work to make sure they do.

Application Challenges

- Identify the links in the supply chain between your employees and the final end user. If your employees can literally shake hands with the customer, great! If not:

- Brainstorm ways for your employees to learn more about the final products/services which they support and implement your best ideas.
- Brainstorm ways to bridge the gap between your employees and their immediate customers and implement your best ideas.

References

1. Kotter, John P. 1996. *Leading Change*. Boston: Harvard Business School Press.
2. Maslow, A.H. 1943. A theory of human motivation. *Psychological Review* 50:370–396.
3. Crabtree, Steve. 2013. Worldwide, 13% of employees are engaged at work. Gallup. http://news.gallup.com/poll/165269/worldwide-employees-engaged-work.aspx (accessed Oct. 5, 2017).
4. Herzberg, Frederick. 1987. One more time: How do you motivate employees? *Harvard Business Review*. September–October 1987.
5. Lencioni, Patrick. 2007. *The Truth About Employee Engagement: A Fable About Addressing the Three Root Causes of Job Misery*. San Francisco. Jossey-Bass.
6. Cranston, Susie and Scott Keller. 2013. Increasing the 'meaning quotient' of work. *McKinsey Quarterly*. January 2013. https://www.mckinsey.com/business-functions /organization/our-insights/increasing-the-meaning-quotient-of-work. (accessed Oct. 12, 2017).
7. https://www.deere.com/en/connect-with-john-deere/gold-key-tours/(accessed Oct. 12, 2017).
8. Steele, Ron. 2013. Deere Gold Key tours impress customers. KWWL. http://www .kwwl.com/story/22527235/2013/06/Thursday/deere-gold-key-tours-impress-customers (accessed Oct. 12, 2017).

Chapter 3

March—Taming the Wilderness: Leadership Behaviors to Build the Culture

Understanding that the appropriate culture is *the* prerequisite—and outcome—for a successful Lean expedition, the logical next question becomes, "So how do I create such a place?"

The good news is that organizational cultures are not dealt out randomly by the business gods, with some organizations inherently blessed and others doomed. Even better, if they so choose, leaders have more sway than others on the culture within the areas for which they are responsible.

Former MIT Sloan School of Management professor Edgar Schein devoted much of his professional life to studying the nuances of organizational culture. One of the more useful components of his work is the identification of various mechanisms which leaders use—both intentionally and unintentionally—to impact culture.[1]

Schein identified six leadership occurrences called "primary embedding mechanisms," which are:

1. What leaders pay attention to, measure, and control on a regular basis
2. Observed criteria by which leaders allocate scare resources
3. How leaders react to critical incidents and organizational crisis

4. Deliberate role modeling, teaching, and coaching
5. Observed criteria by which leaders allocate rewards and status
6. Observed criteria by which leaders recruit, promote, and discipline

According to Schein, these mechanisms always send strong, clear messages. When consistently delivered, the organization's culture will reflect the messages received.

For example, let's assume our leader is frequently asking questions regarding safety (what is measured and paid attention to). She starts her day by stretching with the team (role modeling). Capital is available when an unsafe condition is uncovered (scarce resources). Cutting corners isn't tolerated, even during the busiest days (crisis reaction). We can't help but conclude that our personal safety is really important here.

Now let's imagine a totally different scenario where we frequently see our leader without the appropriate personal safety gear. He walks past machines missing guards because they slow production and his first question at the end of each day is "How many units did you build today?" A high-producing coworker, renowned for taking safety shortcuts, is promoted to supervisor. While none of these messages are intentional, they nonetheless unmistakenly announce that safety isn't a big deal.

Schein also identified six secondary embedding mechanisms:

1. Organizational design and structure
2. Organizational systems and procedures
3. Formal statements of organizational philosophy and values
4. Design of physical space, facades, and buildings
5. Organizational rites and rituals
6. Stories about important people and events

The thing about secondary embedding mechanisms is that they only help establish the desired culture when they are supported by aligned primary embedding mechanisms. If not consistent with primary embedding mechanisms, they only cause confusion and cynicism.

Let's return to the two examples above. In the first case, hanging a framed poster listing safety as one of our core values reinforces the belief that safety is indeed important. A new process introduced to report and address near misses will be well-used because people know issues reported will be taken seriously. The celebration for three years without a lost-time accident will be well attended and meaningful.

Those same three occurrences in the second scenario above won't help to establish a safety culture. Instead, because people observe their leader's behaviors being counter to the stated core values, they will only roll their eyes as the poster is hung, not believing the other values listed. The near-miss reporting program will be doomed. The celebration for three months without a lost-time accident (there's no way they'll make it to three years) will be just an opportunity for a free piece of cake.

Studying the list of primary embedding mechanisms reveals that they are all related to leadership *behaviors*...they are the "walk" rather than the "talk." In fact, they must be *observed* leadership behaviors. Poring over a spreadsheet on accident history in the privacy of one's office doesn't qualify as a primary embedder unless folks see their leader doing something with that data with their own eyes.

What's particularly ironic is that many may perceive the list of secondary embedding mechanisms as "management's work." They create organizational structures, develop systems, and author core values. But real management work is portraying the desired culture consistently in every interaction with employees. That's tough!

Secondary embedding mechanisms aren't bad. When consistent with observed leader behaviors, they enable the organization to more effectively live out the desired culture. When the talk (secondary embedding mechanisms) isn't backed up by the walk (primary embedding mechanisms), however, cynicism reigns. Employees hear observed leader behaviors loud and clear.

This month we'll explore four leadership behaviors that are consistent with creating a culture for Lean success:

1. Listening
2. Serving
3. Welcoming feedback
4. Collaborating and delegating appropriate decision-making

Schein assures us that consistently observed, these behaviors will resonate stronger with employees than any memo or creation of a new Lean promotion department.

Obviously, if managers or supervisors are unable or unwilling to consistently practice these behaviors, they present a serious threat to the success of the expedition. While everyone deserves effective coaching and time to change, those in supervisory roles must be dealt with promptly because of their strong influence over direct reports.

As you're no doubt learning, leading a successful Lean expedition is exhausting (and rewarding). It requires time for reflection in order to recognize progress, identify (and learn from) mistakes, reassess the current situation, and plan next steps. It also necessitates taking time off simply to recharge one's batteries and recommit to the trek. This month we'll dedicate one of our weeks solely for this purpose, a practice we'll continue in each of the following quarters.

Week 9 – Leading and Listening

We all agree that listening is an important leadership skill. At its core, leadership is a relationship between people. Listening is a way of nurturing that relationship as it sends several clear messages:

■ "You are worth my time."
■ "Your ideas are valued and appreciated."
■ "I care about what's going on in your life outside of work."

But is it possible for a leader to listen too much? When is it time to stop listening and start leading? This can be a challenging balance for any leader, but especially for new leaders.

I define leadership as the ability to engage others to leave a known current state and move towards a presumably better (but unknown) future state. That involves anything from relatively benign changes to highly emotional transformations such as how the organization is structured, its products or services, or even its culture.

Leading change within an organization is akin to rolling a large boulder up a hill or changing the direction of rotation on a huge flywheel. First, inertia must be overcome.

In any organization, inertia takes the form of complacency. Members grow comfortable with the status quo. While they may agree the current situation is far from perfect, it's predictable and relatively safe. They likely extrapolate the current situation into the future and see continued safety, perhaps even success for themselves and their coworkers.

Rich dialogue (which always involves listening) therefore plays a critical role *before* a decision is made. Through skillful listening, a leader can ascertain what employees tend to find threatening and why. Some previously unconsidered and valid concerns may be unearthed.

This likewise presents a great opportunity for the leader to begin to illuminate their concerns with the current state and to identify the threats associated with continuing business as usual into the future. Employees' fears regarding future unknowns can be minimized by sharing a vision of what's believed to be possible. Basically, the goal is to decrease the level of discomfort associated with the future and increase the level of uneasiness with the status quo.

During the actual decision-making process, all input gleaned from dialogues should be considered. What were the valid concerns and how will we address them? What were common fears and how will we minimize them?

Following the decision, dialogue again plays a key role to explain the rationale behind it. Proactively addressing concerns identified earlier communicates that they were heard and taken into consideration.

Listening is still important here as well. Everyone processes change differently. Some will need to verbalize their acceptance, others repeat their lingering fears and still others will simply need to vent as a means of letting go of the past. Assuming good listening occurred before the decision, there shouldn't be any major surprises.

Is it possible to listen too much? Technically no. But if a leader allows verbalized, normal fear of change to deter them from taking the organization where they know it must go, they are doing everyone a disservice.

At one end of the listening and leading spectrum is the "don't bother me with facts" unilateral boss. At the other end is the "I don't want to lead…I only want to make everyone happy" pushover.

Both are equally dangerous.

Application Challenges

- Watch Julian Treasure's TED Talk on listening. Practice the techniques discussed.[2]

Week 10 – Servant Leadership (Not an Oxymoron)

Much has been written about the unique Toyota culture which is central to the company's success. And I've read a lot of it. But nothing I read had the impact of listening to Tracey Richardson at a seminar sponsored by the Iowa Lean Consortium.

Richardson, still in her teens, was hired as a line worker as Toyota launched production in its first U.S. plant in Georgetown, Kentucky in 1988. She opted to quit college, deciding that Toyota would be her college education. While that might be a risky decision with most companies, it's turned out pretty nicely for her.

Today she is a successful consultant, thanks to the development she received at Toyota. That says a lot about Richardson's initiative, but volumes about Toyota where the clear expectation is that supervisors spend 50 percent of their time developing employees. I'm guessing that's more than ten times the national average.

The concept that leaders are there for their employees, and not vice versa, is often called servant leadership. It turns the traditional organizational chart upside down, placing frontline workers at the top. These are the folks "shaking hands with customers" every day, either by building and packaging the product in the case of manufacturing or directly taking care of customers in service industries.

First-line supervisors and support staff are next on the inverted org chart, providing whatever frontline workers need to get the job done. That includes personal development, so that employees' capacity to solve problems and add more value increases. Likewise, managers are listed below supervisors and on down to the CEO. Each subsequent layer is responsible for developing and serving those above them on the chart.

As Brian Dieter, CEO at Mary Greeley Medical Center, tells employees, "There are only two jobs here…taking care of patients and taking care of those who take care of patients."

Unfortunately, on-the-job trappings often increase with each subsequent promotion. One physically moves from the floor to a desk job, then to a personal office, next to an office with an administrative assistant to filter "interruptions" and finally to a mahogany boardroom.

It's not surprising then that many new supervisors and managers physically and mentally separate themselves from the very people they are asked to lead. They fall into the trap of believing they have "earned" the right to exercise power due to their location on the ladder.

It's therefore critical that organizations select supervisors and managers based on their observed ability to help others. Expectations for developing employees should be clearly communicated and measured, including how much time is physically spent each day where the work is performed.

Organizations must challenge their policies to ensure that they are supportive of a servant leadership philosophy. Increased pay is appropriate for a skilled supervisor who increases the effectiveness of several employees. But other more visible distinctions which favor management should be discouraged.

For example, my disdain for executive parking spaces rivals my feelings for disco music. Fortunately, both lost favor in most places by the 1980s. But Mary Greeley Medical Center took it a step further. When an expansion project temporarily reduced parking capacity, the hospital required its managers to park at a lot two blocks off-site. That sent a strong message to frontline employees that they were valued, especially in light of Iowa's often less-than-ideal weather.

OK, all this is nice, but does it pay off? It certainly has for Toyota.

In his bestselling book *Good to Great*, author Jim Collins identifies seven distinguishing factors of companies that were able to sustain outstanding results for several years. He calls one of those factors "Level 5 Leaders," those possessing both "personal humility" and "professional will."[3]

These are not celebrity leaders whose companies go into decline when they move on. They are more concerned with building a team than with taking credit. They are more apt to ask the right questions and develop people than provide answers. They are akin to a humble all-star offensive lineman, not an outspoken quarterback or wide receiver.

Whenever I hear a leader explain how much their organization has grown since they came on board, I gently remind them that the true measure of their effectiveness will be how much it grows in the ten years after they leave.

Application Challenges

- Read Chapter 2 ("Level 5 Leadership") in Jim Collins' *Good to Great*.[3]
- Monitor how much time you spend in a typical week developing your employees. Set an improvement goal and monitor progress.

Week 11 – Taking Time Off (Spring Break!)

A hot topic in the business news recently is the trend of companies offering employees "unlimited vacation." Did you flinch the first time you heard that? (I did.)

But as Albert Einstein stated, "If at first the idea is not absurd, then there is no hope for it."[4] This doesn't mean that every crazy idea should be pursued, but rather that significant, positive change starts with ideas that are initially outside of our existing paradigms.

Won't people take advantage of the situation? In *Love and Profit*, former Meredith CEO James Autry defines bad policies as "those written to keep everyone from doing what only a few people are going to do…and they're going to do it anyway."[5] In other words, those "special" people will provide you with multiple reasons to fire them.

For *most* of us, when and how much time off we take is dictated more by workload and perhaps personal situations outside of our control (e.g., illness) than by the number of hours we've accrued. Tax accountants know a spring break trip is not in the cards for them regardless of how many vacation hours they have in the bank.

In fact, opponents rightfully suggest the "unlimited vacation" policy can be manipulative if the culture is one of overloading employees with work and making folks feel guilty for taking time off. They point to data from multiple organizations that implemented the flexible policy and had employees actually take less time off.

Thus, for a win-win situation to exist, the organization must truly value, preach, and (most importantly) demonstrate the value of recharging. This includes leaders modeling time off.

The benefits of an unlimited vacation policy for organizations can be significant, both in measurable and intangible areas:

- Savings associated with not buying back unused time off from employees who were already paid full wages while working at less-than-peak levels because their batteries were drained
- Savings associated with not tracking and categorizing time off (sick, bereavement, jury duty, vacation, etc.) to the fractional hour
- Increased innovation and vigor resulting from physically and emotionally rested employees

Perhaps even more important than how much time is taken off is *how* that time off is actually used. Many times I've shaken my head in sadness while observing some poor soul lost in their laptop at the beach or the pool. The increased capability of smart phones increases the subtlety as well as the frequency of this condition. That's not time off, but rather exotic telecommuting.

Several years ago while on vacation, I dove into my email on a Thursday afternoon in hopes of managing the backlog I would return to the following Monday. From that moment on, I transitioned out of time off mode to work mode. "Never again!" I swore.

As a sole proprietor now, I confess that I've modified that a bit. Prior to leaving, I let existing clients know that I will be gone but available via cell phone in case of a true emergency. They respect that; in eight years I recall a single call (and it was a true emergency). I quickly check my email inbox daily simply to determine if a new client is "entering the shop for the first time." If so, I send them a short note explaining the situation and that I will get back to them.

Time off offers everyone—managers and employees—unique opportunities to see the big picture. It's why strategic planning sessions are best held off-site. There's something about sitting on a deck at sunset and enjoying a unique landscape that's conducive to clear thinking, to exploring high level strategic questions:

- Are the most important relationships in my life growing stronger or weaker?
- How is my work/life balance scale currently tilted?
- Is the vision for my company (department) still valid?
- Are the strategies for reaching that vision working?

Make sure that you and your employees are truly taking time away from work to recharge. The organization with survive the week (even two) and will be much stronger long term.

Application Challenges

- Schedule time off multiple times each year; plan adventures that fit your budget.
- Use a simple check sheet to monitor how many times you violate time off by checking email, taking a phone call, etc. Categorize the violations and create an improvement plan.
- Read Stephen Covey's *First Things First*[6] or the corresponding chapter ("Habit 3: Put First Things First") in Covey's *The Seven Habits of Highly Effective People: Powerful Lessons in Personal Change.*[7]
- Take advantage of your time away to identify the important roles you fulfill in your life (e.g., spouse, parent, supervisor, etc.) and set goals for each role.

Week 12 – Telling It Like It Is

There's an old Sicilian proverb that states only your real friends will tell you when your face is dirty. Had they already been invented, this proverb no doubt would have been revised to only your real friends will tell you when your zipper is down.

As a leader within your organization, it's important that you have people who care enough about you and the organization to tell you when your face is dirty or you are experiencing a wardrobe malfunction.

In my role as a production manager, I was fortunate to have Myron and Bill. Both were supervisors, which meant they reported to the team leaders who reported to me. On many an occasion, I found them waiting for me outside my office, soon after a key announcement or decision.

"Okay guys, what did I do this time?"

They would then describe how the recent message had been misconstrued by a few workers. On other occasions they would patiently explain an unintended, yet potential, ramification of the new decision. Their feedback was never judgmental but instead factual and always eye-opening for me.

Then we would discuss damage control. Often this was as simple as me having one-on-one discussions with the few required to clarify the message. Other times it meant tweaking the solution to address the potential harmful consequences.

In short, Bill and Myron saved my bacon on a number of occasions. The emperor could have used both of them on his cabinet prior to modeling his new clothes in public.

In hindsight, there are a number of factors inherent to a culture which allows this type of feedback to occur.

A rigid hierarchical structure which demands that communication only follow "proper protocol" almost certainly squelches valuable feedback. In my experience, there are two reasons people go around their direct supervisors. Either the message doesn't involve them (as was the case described above) or (more likely) they know from experience that the feedback will not be positively received or acted upon by their supervisor.

In the latter case, the bypassed supervisor is typically paranoid because they lack skills and confidence in many areas. They attempt to protect themselves by hoping to filter messages headed to the top.

Healthy feedback organizations make it clear that thinking isn't the sole domain of management. Employees at every level of the organization are challenged to create the next great idea...or to simply identify a small improvement to their part of the process.

Another requirement for a healthy feedback culture is strong teamwork. Implicit trust existed during those conversations in my office. Bill and Myron knew that my goof-ups were honest human mistakes. I knew that their feedback was not politically motivated. It was clear that we were wearing the same jerseys.

Finally, feedback should almost always be accompanied with an action plan. These aren't esoteric conversations. The ultimate reward to those providing feedback is to act upon it.

Here's a list of questions to assess your role in establishing a healthy feedback culture:

- Are you approachable to all levels of employees within your organization? Do you approach them and get to know them as people first?
- How do you respond when the feedback is less than pleasant? Do you listen to hear the intended message, rationalize, or get defensive?
- Do those brave and insightful souls who bother to give you feedback know how much you appreciate them? Do they come back?
- How often do you act upon feedback? Do you close the loop with those providing the feedback so they know what you did with it?

My wish is that every leader is lucky (or skilled) enough to have a number of Bills and Myrons. Nurturing such a culture will save you from a number of dirty faces...and much worse.

Application Challenges

- Do you already have folks within your organization that care enough about you to provide honest feedback?
  - If so, take time today to tell them how much you appreciate their insight.
  - If not, identify a couple of people that can fulfill this role and ask them.
- Think about the last time you received honest, but less than favorable feedback from someone who is subordinate in your organization. Did your response make it likely that feedback will be given in the future?

Week 13 – The Power of "We"

Shortly after I began consulting, I was having a conversation with a client when they interrupted mid-sentence:

"You know what I like about you?" they asked.
"What's that?" (I was sporting a dashing new haircut.)
"You always talk about 'we,' like you're a part of our team, not some outsider simply coming in to tell us what to do."

At first, I was somewhat taken aback that such a seemingly minor detail warranted feedback, however, over the course of the last decade, I received similar comments from several clients.

Upon further thought, I shouldn't have been surprised. As leaders, *how* we lead is just as important to those following as the desired destination. A quote often attributed to Theodore Roosevelt perhaps says it best, "Nobody cares how much you know, until they know how much you care."[8]

Utilizing inclusive pronouns (we, us, our) rather than exclusive (you, I, your, mine) is a small but powerful mechanism for leaders. It sends a clear message that "we're in this together."

Obviously, when recognizing someone for a job well done, it's more appropriate to use "you." Likewise, when discussing a shortcoming on your part, it's best to own it with "I" or "my."

Language is a telltale indicator for me when interviewing candidates, especially managers. I tend to keep a mental scorecard of the candidate's use of "I" versus "we" when discussing prior accomplishments. Too many "I did..." statements and the deeds themselves—regardless of how impressive—take a backseat to my conclusion that they are not a team player.

Of course, words are just icing on the cake. The real proof is in how the leader leads. Perhaps there is no better indication of this than how decisions are made.

A leader's decision-making style impacts whether and to what extent employees sign up to follow. When an authoritative style is used, the direction is simply ordered up. The best we can hope for is that folks will be compliant simply out of respect for rank.

If a persuasive style is used, the leader still makes the decision unilaterally, perhaps with input from others. They take the time to explain the reasoning behind their decision in hopes of winning over the hearts and heads of followers. Well done, persuasion results in the conversion of some compliant followers to committed and some resistant non-followers to compliant followers as compared to merely ordering up the decision.

When a collaborative style is used, leaders actively involve followers by gathering input, asking for their recommendation and perhaps delegating the actual decision. Properly applied in the appropriate situations, this leads to high levels of followers committed to the decision's success...they own it.

Obviously, the situation dictates which decision-making style is appropriate. A crisis may not allow the time necessary for a healthy collaborative debate. The selection of potential choices may be so undesirable, such as a layoff situation, that commitment is not likely to be gained even through collaboration.

It serves a leader well to move as high on the participatory scale as the situation allows. In addition to increasing the percentage of committed followers to the decision, involving others in appropriate decisions is a powerful development mechanism. The level of trust involved and the opportunity for employees to use their unique talents means they are operating at the highest levels of Maslow's pyramid.

Finally, developing employees to confidently make decisions is essential to relieving leaders of unnecessary duties so that they can focus on more strategic activities. It's vital to building a strong, committed team where "we" is the appropriate pronoun.

Application Challenges

- Monitor your language; are your pronouns inclusive (we, us, our) or exclusive (you, I, your, mine)?
- What decision do your regularly make that can be delegated to a capable team member? For that decision, transition from decision-maker to coach for the employee assuming responsibility for it. Once successfully transitioned, repeat.

References

1. Schein, Edgar H., 2010. *Organizational Culture and Leadership*. San Francisco: John Wiley & Sons, Inc.
2. https://www.ted.com/talks/julian_treasure_5_ways_to_listen_better. (accessed Feb. 17, 2018).
3. Collins, Jim. 2001. *Good to Great: Why Some Companies Make the Leap…and Others Don't*. New York: HarperCollins Publishers Inc.
4. https://www.goodreads.com/quotes/110518-if-at-first-the-idea-is-not-absurd-then-there. (accessed Oct. 12, 2017).
5. Autry, J.A. 1991. *Love and Profit: The Art of Caring Leadership*. New York: Avon Books.
6. Covey, Stephen R., S. Roger Merrill and Rebecca R. Merrill. 1994. *First Things First*. New York: Fireside.
7. Covey, Stephen R. 1989. *The Seven Habits of Highly Effective People: Powerful Lessons in Personal Change*. New York: Free Press.
8. http://www.theodorerooseveltcenter.org/Learn-About-TR/TR-Quotes?page=3. (accessed Dec. 23, 2017).

Chapter 4

April—Living in the Wilderness: Rounding – An Intentional Habit for Culture Change

During March we explored four leadership behaviors that, observed regularly, are consistent with building a Lean culture:

1. Listening
2. Serving and developing employees
3. Welcoming feedback
4. Collaborating and delegating appropriate decision-making

Practicing these behaviors over time ultimately leads to employees that feel valued and connected to the organization. They care enough to point out barriers to serving customers and are willing, confident, and competent addressing those barriers when within their sphere of influence.

This month we'll introduce a formal mechanism for practicing the key behaviors—rounding on employees. Modeled after the regular, frequent checks which nurses perform on their patients, many healthcare facilities now document standard work for nurses, defining rounding frequency and the actual steps to be taken when visiting a patient.[1]

Perhaps you're already occasionally meeting one-on-one with employees. If so, great! Rounding requires these visits to be intentional (i.e., scheduled) and preferably within the employee's work area. The appropriate frequency will be dictated by the speed at which work conditions can change. Two or three times per day may be apt for a high-volume manufacturing environment; once a week for an engineering team.

Just as a spaceship must overcome the gravitational pull of the earth in order to successfully reach orbit, so a supervisor must overcome the invisible force field surrounding their office to successfully lead. While a planet's gravitation force is proportional to its mass, the pull of one's office increases with posh, its distance from those supervised, and the amount of administrational paperwork for which the supervisor is responsible.

Perhaps no factor limits a manager's success more than their inability or unwillingness to leave their office and visit the action. Making a commitment to employee rounding provides the energy to overcome the lure of the office.

Week 14 – Creating Red Flag Mechanisms While Rounding

The concept of management by walking/wandering around (MBWA) is thought to have begun at Hewlett-Packard in the 1970s. MBWA went mainstream in 1982 with Tom Peters and Robert Waterman's classic book *In Search of Excellence: Lessons from America's Best Run Companies*.[2] The basic idea, as the name implies, is management making spontaneous, random, and unstructured checks on people, machines, and processes.

While I certainly support the idea of supervisors regularly spending face-to-face time with the people they manage where the work is completed (not the manager's office), I have some misgivings with the concept of MBWA.

First, supervisors are among the busiest people on the planet. Thus, expecting them to "spontaneously" visit the troops when they find time is practically akin to ordering it not to happen.

Second, over the course of the past 40 years or so, I'd like to think we've advanced beyond unstructured wandering. That seems a bit too hit-and-miss for me.

The practice of employee rounding adds structure or standard to spending time with employees at the point of value creation. These include:

■ Intentionally scheduling time for rounding to increase the odds that it occurs. This doesn't mean that it must be predictable ("Well, it's 10:28; the boss should be coming around the corner right about...now!")
■ Connecting with employees on a personal level. Not with a generic "How's it going?" but rather something specific like, "Have you got a photo of that 12-point buck I've been hearing about?"

- Consistently asking questions to understand if there are barriers to the employee serving their customers, if a coworker should be recognized for going the extra mile, and if they have any ideas for improvement.
- Documenting main ideas so they don't get lost; these become topics for future rounding discussions.

If barriers or improvement ideas are identified, it's important that resolution remain with the employee if they are capable. And most employees are typically more capable than given credit for or they sometimes want to admit. Solving problems provides growth opportunities and frees the supervisor for their most important responsibilities.

Which brings us back to time management. How does a busy supervisor consistently find time to round?

Let's start by reducing two of the biggest non-value-added time suckers for any supervisor...administrational (i.e., paper) work and crisis clean-up. Be hypersensitive regarding administrational work required of supervisors. Ensure administrational processes are streamlined so supervisor involvement is minimal. Where possible, delegate administrational duties to clerical assistants or subordinates. Having employees responsible for monitoring their own performance is more effective anyway.

By being on top of things, both personnel- and process-related, problems can be identified sooner and the number of crises reduced. In addition to saving time, this eliminates the need to apologize to a customer or explain to management why numbers aren't acceptable, among any supervisor's least favorite activities.

To spot problems early and make rounding most effective, create a series of mini-feedback systems (flags) which provide instantaneous feedback on whether things are in control (green flag) or out of control (red flag). Examples of potential red flag mechanisms might include:

- Is everyone wearing the appropriate personal protective equipment (PPE)?
- Do employees appear comfortable (physically and emotionally)?
- Are people working on the right jobs?
- Are bottlenecks protected (staffed, work staged in front of them)?
- Are standards being followed (e.g., are tools and electronic files stored in the agreed upon location, are the correct process steps being followed)?
- Are visual metrics up-to-date and are results as expected?
- Audit various machine parameters; are they within the proper tolerances?
- Request a quality check; is it completed properly with the anticipated result?
- Do things look, sound, smell, and feel the way they should?

If things are in control, a typical rounding discussion can occur. If not, immediate action must first be taken to get things back on track.

Realize that *really* understanding what's going on with people and processes is *the* most important priority for any supervisor. Intentional (scheduled) employee rounding is simply a way of putting first things first.

Application Challenges

- Determine the appropriate frequency to meet with each of your employees. How much time is required to have a short but quality discussion on the status of work and also to touch base with them personally?
- Identify what you can stop doing or delegate in order to begin rounding on your employees. Intentionally schedule time for this important activity on your calendar.
- Make a list of potential red flag mechanisms as you round on your employees.

Week 15 – Sweating the Soft Stuff

My friend Marie returned from the 2014 Psychotherapy Networker Symposium with an audio file from a presentation entitled *Attachment Leadership* and suggested, "You need to listen to this."[3]

Now I try to be pretty open-minded on where my next lesson might originate. But I was a bit skeptical that something from a psychotherapy symposium would find usefulness in my work with clients.

I've listened to the file three times.

The presentation was a collaboration between Donald Rheem, an organizational consultant, and his wife Kathryn, a psychotherapist. They point out that few management fads are grounded in science with empirical data to support them. As a recovering engineer, they had my attention.

According to the Rheems, every employee comes to work every day with discretionary effort. They decide, consciously or subconsciously, how much effort they're going to put forth. How much discretionary effort they expend is directly proportional to their level of engagement.

A distribution curve for the level of employee engagement can be constructed, just like any other variable which describes us (height, IQ, etc.). At the low end of the curve are a minority of employees classified as "actively disengaged." This group can be described by a number of factors, including high absenteeism, high accident rates, and low productivity, typically putting forth only a fraction of a full day's effort.

Next higher on the distribution are the majority of employees, split between those classified as "somewhat disengaged" and "somewhat engaged" with productivity factors slightly below and above 100 percent, respectively. Finally, at the top end is another minority called "actively engaged" with productivity far exceeding their peers. These are the folks that identify waste, go the extra mile to serve customers and solve problems.

Each company, even each department, has its own unique employee engagement distribution. A primary factor defining that unique distribution is the unique culture of the company, (or microculture for a department) with culture being defined simply as the answer to, "What does it really feel like to work here?"

The default for new employees is to enter on the positive (engaged) side of the distribution, but over time they tend to disperse across the unique curve for their work unit. The implications here are enormous as the productivity of the actively engaged is several times that of the actively disengaged.

So, the natural question becomes "What can managers do to create a culture conducive to actively engaged employees?" To answer that, the Rheems turned to the physiology of the brain.

Throughout evolution, survival of the human race relied on its ability to cooperate as a tribe for safety, connection, and the ability to share the load. This is now hardwired into our brains. Today's tribe is the workplace and we still yearn for safety (albeit more emotional than physical), connection, and load sharing.

The primitive center of our brain (limbic brain) is hyperactive and focused on safety. It's constantly asking "What's next?" and "How am I doing?" It is constantly running in the background, requires little fuel, and is not especially bright.

The creative and problem-solving portion of our brain is the prefrontal cortex. Because it requires great energy to run, it is often on standby unless called on by the limbic brain due to a safety alert or it is motivated to solve a problem.

The presenters provide an excellent analogy of driving a car along the same road but under vastly different weather conditions. During a beautiful, sunny summer day we arrive rejuvenated by the drive; on an icy, stormy winter night, we are exhausted. The difference is not in the amount of physical effort, but rather the degree to which we taxed our prefrontal cortex.

That same taxing occurs when employees are consumed by worry at work. Conversely, supervisors free up the creativity centers in their employees' brains for productive work when they provide a safe haven in which people feel connected and work is fairly shared.

A safe haven shouldn't be confused with a coddling zone, but rather an environment free of unnecessary drama and guided by a supervisor whose actions are consistent and predictable. A place where one feels genuinely appreciated and challenged to grow for both the benefit of themselves and the tribe.

Employee rounding provides a regular framework for building that caring and supportive relationship. It sends a clear message that "You are worth my time" and that "Your work is important." It provides opportunities to discuss and hopefully address potentially stressful issues while they are still small. Finally, it also allows one to challenge and guide employees to use their creativity to solve problems that impact their work, resulting in increased engagement and discretionary effort.

Application Challenges

- List what you know about each of your employees (name of their significant other, children's names, interests, hobbies, etc.). Use these as discussion starters when rounding.
- Understand your employees' peeves, personal challenges, and stressors in order to be empathetic.

Week 16 – Keeping Score

Let's focus on one of Patrick Lencioni's root causes for job misery—referred to as "immeasurement" or the absence of pertinent measurements for one to assess how things are going.[4]

We are a society comfortable with measurement. Listen in on the conversations in any break room and you'll hear all sorts of numbers being shared:

- "I shot a 43 on the back nine last night…"
- "We averaged 57 miles per hour on the way out to Denver…"
- "That walleye on the left weighed just under seven pounds…"
- "My Civic is getting 36 miles per gallon…"
- "My grandson Michael scored a 30 on his ACT test…"

After lunch is over, the majority of these same employees return to jobs devoid of measures, save for perhaps a cursory count of how many times they completed their primary work activity. The result is that employees, not to mention their supervisors, have little objective data with which to assess one's process or opportunities for improvement.

Consider that the average high school basketball player has considerably more tangible data available to them than the typical worker. Now consider the potential consequences of problems for each; while the athlete may lose a game or some playing time the employee stands to lose a livelihood.

So how does one go about developing an environment of healthy measurement? The first step is to begin regularly sharing the overall performance or score of the organization. This should be a balanced set of metrics covering all of the critical aspects of the organization—safety, quality, delivery, and some type of financial measurement (profit, cost, or productivity). While it may be prudent to use discretion in sharing financial information within a private business, a metric which protects the owner's interests yet is meaningful to employees can be developed with some careful thought.

Once the organization's overall measurements have been established, work teams and even individuals can be guided to identify local measurements which support the global metrics. For example, if the organization is tracking customer complaints or defects, order entry personnel should monitor their error rate for orders containing bad or missing information which result in errant or delayed shipments.

Consideration should be given to design metrics so that employees can easily garner the necessary data in as close to real time as possible. With a bit of creativity, a simple, clear, and visual scoreboard can be established within the work area with employees responsible for daily updates. Goals should be included on the scoreboard and celebrated when they are attained.

Discussing the score is therefore a natural discussion topic for employee rounding. Does everyone know how the organization is doing on top level measures? Do we understand how our local numbers support the organization's values? Are there ideas for improving the local results or barriers to improvement?

One important word of caution: Performance is almost always a stronger reflection of the processes used to perform work rather than of the workers themselves. For example, try as I may this past winter, I just couldn't match my neighbor's ability to clear a driveway of snow. That's because his process involved a two-stage, five-horsepower blower, while my process used a single-stage, three-horsepower wimp (and a shovel when it could no longer clear the snow bank).

As fellow consultant Ken Miller eloquently advises, we measure to determine why, not who.[5] Holding people accountable for results in a broken process or a process over which they have no control is a recipe for gaming the system.

This means that certainly managers (and preferably employees) must be trained to identify and know how to react—or not react—appropriately. Common cause variation is the random variation inherent in the system's design. Let's assume we monitor fuel efficiency of a bus that drives a specific route. Gas mileage on any given day will vary based on a number of factors outside of the driver's control such as ambient temperature (which impacts tire pressure and whether heating or air conditioning is required), traffic, passenger load, etc. Reacting to changes in common cause variation is akin to rewarding or punishing a child for their height.

Special cause variation is that attributable to an identifiable external change to the system. Returning to our bus, examples of special cause variation in fuel efficiency might be a tire going flat, an engine malfunction, or a bad tank of fuel. Skillfully and quickly identifying from the data when we are outside of common cause variation and in the realm of special cause variation allows us to quickly identify problems and increase the chances of finding the root cause ("This all started about the time I last filled up.").

When employees begin constantly thinking of ways to improve the processes they use to perform work, both they and their organization benefit. Knowing the score is the first step towards improving it.

Application Challenges

- Identify the top three to five organizational objectives which your team impacts. For each of these objectives, determine the level of performance required by your team to help the organization meet its goal.
- Develop a visual metric to track local performance for each objective, understanding that sustainment of the metric requires that the data must be very easy to attain. Well-designed graphs will make it instantaneously obvious from several feet away whether we are tracking on target or not.
- If you are not already familiar with common cause and special cause variation and the appropriate management of each, read Chapter 8 of W. Edwards Deming's *Out of the Crisis.*[6]

Week 17 – Getting Out of the Office to Solve Problems

Developing robust personal and professional relationships with employees is the primary impetus for rounding. Creating and monitoring visual cues, including out-of-control data points, allows us to more quickly identify budding problems before they become a crisis. There's also another reason to get out of the office and visit the place where value is added, which I will describe with a brief anecdote:

Epic flooding of the Missouri River occurred along Iowa's western border during 2011. I followed the news with more than a passing interest. As an engineer, I knew that in order to shut down an interstate highway, an event was occurring that exceeded the careful calculations completed when the highway was constructed half a century ago.

What really struck me, however, was the predicted duration of the disaster. As the situation unfolded in early June, forecasts were calling for flooding to persist throughout August and perhaps even until the end of September.

My first reaction was, "How can this be? Someone must have really screwed up managing the flows. And there's no way those duration forecasts can be right. Someone's off by a decimal point." (Notice how my first reaction focused on "Who?" I'm not proud of that.)

As a native of Iowa's east coast, I knew big river flooding. ("Heck, if you think this is bad you should have seen '65!" was a common refrain in my hometown of Dubuque.)

Then in late June my wife Janet and I went on a vacation to Yellowstone National Park. From the time we crossed the Missouri River at Chamberlain, South Dakota every single tributary from the roaring Yellowstone River to the tiniest mountain stream was out of its banks. Furthermore, at elevation the snow waiting to join the deluge exceeded anything we had seen in Iowa from the worst February blizzard.

In short, I thought I knew big rivers. But after visiting the actual site it became obvious that the Missouri and Mississippi Rivers are entirely different animals when it comes to their potential for flooding Iowa for an extended period of time. A quick review of maps after returning home confirmed that the Missouri's watershed upstream of Iowa is significantly greater and includes elevated snowpack.

My flooding experience is similar to a trap that frequently snares successful managers and supervisors. Many attribute career advancement to their ability to resolve a past problem using a perceived unique skill.

It's only natural then that they continue to look for other instances to utilize their perceived forte. In short, they mistakenly assume that the solution successfully applied to a past problem can be effectively extrapolated to every new issue which bears some resemblance, similar to my "I know big river flooding!"

Financial market literature refers to extrapolation bias, the tendency of our minds to see a pattern when in fact one doesn't exist. Vic, one of my first bosses, perhaps said it best: "When you assume, you make an ass of u and me."

Given that our human tendencies are working against us, how do we guard against the urge to jump to an inaccurate conclusion or ineffective solution?

First and foremost, get out of the office and visit the site of the issue. Visit firsthand with the people who deal directly with the problem day in and day out. What have they observed? What do they think is going on? View it with your own eyes if at all possible.

The Japanese refer to this as going to the *gemba* or the "real place." This is similar to a detective visiting the scene of the crime or my visit to the headwaters of the Missouri.

Be aware that newly minted college graduates, as well as recently promoted shop floor personnel, often feel they've earned their office. Make sure that they clearly understand that they earn their keep by supporting those people who perform the real work of the organization, those that pay the bills.

Don't exacerbate that tendency with luxurious offices located far from where the work occurs. Taj Mahal offices only benefit the building contractor.

Ensure that your organization embraces a formal problem-solving *process* to methodically identify and prove the root cause(s) of a well-defined problem, using data whenever possible. Eight Disciplines (8D), A3, and Six Sigma's DMAIC are all proven methodologies which encourage analytic proof rather than merely opinions.

Finally, develop a culture where it is encouraged to make problems visible rather than sweeping them under the carpet. Little problems ignored, tend to grow into a flood.

Application Challenges

- Select and practice a formal problem-solving *process* (8D, A3, DMAIC), even on routine problems, so that the process becomes a habit.
- Each of the aforementioned tools utilizes a rigorous problem definition step. Make "let's go see firsthand or at least talk to those who have" part of your problem definition.

References

1. Studer, Quint. 2008. *Results That Last: Hardwiring Behaviors That Will Take Your Company to the Top.* Hoboken, NJ: John Wiley & Sons, Inc.
2. Peters, Thomas J. and Robert H. Waterman. 2006. *In Search of Excellence: Lessons from America's Best Run Companies.* New York: HarperCollins Publishers Inc.
3. Rheem, Donald and Kathryn Rheem. 2014. *Attachment Leadership.* 2014 Psychotherapy Networker Symposium.
4. Lencioni, Patrick. 2007. *The Truth About Employee Engagement: A Fable About Addressing the Three Root Causes of Job Misery.* San Francisco: Jossey-Bass.
5. Miller, Ken. 2014. *Extreme Government Makeover: Increasing Our Capacity to Do More Good.* Washington, DC: Governing Books.
6. Deming, W. Edwards. 2000. *Out of the Crisis.* Cambridge, MA: The MIT Press.

Chapter 5

May—Choosing the Right People for the Expedition: Building a Strong Team

So far, we've focused entirely on the leader-manager's role, which includes:

- The need for their honest assessment and motivation to endure the challenges associated with leading a change effort.
- Their unique role in nurturing the appropriate culture prior to (or at least in conjunction with) introducing tools.
- Four fundamental leader behaviors which positively influence progress towards the required culture.
- A key habit for leaders to embrace which provides a regular framework for practicing the four fundamental behaviors.

But great teams require excellent coaches *and* talented, engaged players. This month we turn our attention to selecting the right employees, including those that will supervise others.

While compromise is a necessary skill for successful leaders, it can be hazardous when applied to hiring new employees or selecting supervisors. The need to fill an open position or the tightness of the labor market is never so great as to justify overlooking a misalignment between a candidate and the organization's stated values.

Hiring and promoting decisions dwarf almost all others in both the message they send to the organization as well as the magnitude and longevity of their impact.

They are a rare opportunity to metaphorically grab a megaphone and announce, "Here's what we mean by (fill in the blank with your organization's values)!"

Nowhere is this more critical than when selecting those who will supervise others. Recall Schein's advice from March that the observed criteria by which leaders recruit, promote, and discipline is a primary embedding mechanism for how leaders influence culture.[1] Appointing a lousy supervisor for say, a dozen employees, can arguably carry almost as much weight as hiring a dozen substandard employees.

While not irreversible, hiring and promoting the wrong person will require significant personal attention and anxiety. Inertia all but guarantees they will stay in the position longer than justified before a correction is made. The result is almost assuredly a net negative for the organization, worse than if the opening was left unfilled.

Your recruitment, hiring, and promotion processes should therefore be as robust as those used to provide products and services to your customers.

Week 18 – A Most Critical Decision

Few management decisions carry as much impact as deciding who to hire. Hiring the right person results in a daily affirmation of a wise choice. A poor hire, on the other hand, requires an inordinate amount of attention, demoralizes teammates, and may eventually call for an unpleasant termination.

The hiring challenge is complicated by the fact that most candidates are on their absolute best behavior; true identities are well-hidden behind an interview façade. Nonetheless, there are time-tested techniques which greatly improve the odds of making a sound decision.

First of all, employing a team approach increases the likelihood of a quality decision. A team tends to negate the potential for the decision being overly influenced by a sole interviewer's halo effect which is a positive bias resulting from a shared trait. For example, an interviewer's assessment is positively biased towards the candidate because they attended the same school, belonged to the same sorority, were both Eagle Scouts, etc. If your organization is very small or you can't involve coworkers in the hiring decision for whatever reason, form a small interview team of trusted outside colleagues who understand your organization.

Gather the team together a couple of days prior to the interview to develop a game plan. Each interviewer should be assigned a couple of designated focus areas and encouraged to develop open-ended, thought-provoking questions which allow them to deeply evaluate the candidate in those areas.

What's the source of these focus areas? They should be a direct reflection of your organization's core values. Hiring new employees and evaluating current ones are two primary activities for bringing core values to life. If core values are not key criteria in your hiring and evaluation processes, there's a good chance that they are little more than ambiguous concepts framed on the wall.

Below are some interview techniques to consider:

- I like to lead off with a question regarding the three things the candidate values most. Their answer generally indicates how open and honest they are and therefore, how much I can trust them during the remainder of the interview. It's my calibration question.
- When time management skills are critical to the job, I've had great success with handing the candidate a list of ten questions and asking them to lead the conversation. If they're still responding to the first question 20 minutes into a scheduled 45-minute interview, they're not the right person.
- If attention to detail is important or your organization values cleanliness and orderliness, have someone discretely check out the candidate's car (assuming they drove their own) for those qualities.
- Scheduling lunch with the candidate's potential peers works well. The informal atmosphere often leads to the candidate letting their guard down and responding more honestly to questions.
- Steal a trick from the TV detective Columbo and ask an important question as if it's an afterthought while wrapping up. Again, this may lead to a less rehearsed answer.

A report-out meeting with the interview team should be scheduled on the same day as the interview so that it's still fresh in everyone's mind. Avoid groupthink by asking each team member to come to the meeting with their recommendation on the candidate. A fun way to quickly assess responses is to have all interviewers simultaneously bounce their fist into their hand two times (á la rock-paper-scissors) and then cast their vote with a thumbs-up, thumbs-down, or thumbs-sideways.

Any negative or neutral votes should be judiciously explored via discussion. Reaching team consensus prior to discounting any highlighted concerns is warranted before proceeding with an offer. This is because the interview setting may likely be the best you will ever see the candidate again. Countless managers have later lamented that an employee's now glaring weakness was identified as a yellow flag during the interview but rationalized away.

Application Challenges

- Seriously consider using a team approach to interviewing if not already. In addition to making better decisions, involvement with the hiring process will increase the team's ownership to ensure the new hire is successful.
- If your organization has identified core values, insist that these are heavy criteria during the interview process.

Week 19 – Tweet This!

At the risk of sounding like a bit of a curmudgeon, I'm concerned that a significant subset of those entering the workforce may be missing a key skill—the ability to interact directly with other human beings. Here are my data points:

According to a 2014 study published in the *Journal of Behavioral Addictions*, female students at Baylor University spend ten hours per day on their phones.[2] Ten hours! The same study reported that male students at Baylor spend eight hours daily with their heads in their phones. That's more time than I spent with my head buried in a pillow during college.

A client recently reported that they were interviewing to replace a professional position in which direct, tactful communication with customers was a critical job requirement. They filtered resumes and invited multiple candidates for face-to-face interviews, each scheduled for 45 minutes. None of the candidates were comfortable and skilled enough in dialogue to utilize the entire 45 minutes. The shortest lasted seven minutes!

At an industry conference, colleagues from two highly respected manufacturing firms shared unsolicited stories with me within an hour of each other complaining of their professional employees with an inability or unwillingness to collaborate with other departments. Specifically, product designs were being thrown over the wall and causing major issues in manufacturing. Mind you, these weren't occurring at start-ups but rather company names that anyone recognizes.

Wait a minute, how can that be? This problem was solved 20 years ago. Just put a manufacturing expert on the design team. Teach the design engineers the importance of interacting with the factory. At that point I was interrupted, "Rick, I need to literally grab a couple of my engineers by the elbow and tell them, 'We're going to visit a place called the factory.' I swear the only interacting they do with others is with their fingers on their phone."

With so many potential employees entering the workforce with cellphone addictions, it becomes important to screen for this condition. Unlike other addictions, a simple urine or blood test has not been developed. We'll have to get a bit more creative.

Include the receptionist as part of the interview team. Ask them to observe the candidate while waiting for their contact to arrive. Are they curious? Candidates who browse the lobby and peruse company literature earn bonus points. Those who strike up a conversation with the receptionist or other visitors receive double bonus points! Monitor the candidate's time from entering the building until reaching for their phone. Eliminate anyone who has their nose in their phone while addressing the receptionist.

Monitor phone presence during the interview. Candidates whose phones are totally invisible (visually and audibly) receive bonus points. Deduct points for each vibrating tone received during the interview, double deductions for each audible ring tone.

Consider intentionally asking closed-ended questions. This goes against traditional interviewing advice, but we're trying to discern if the candidate is comfortable and skilled in dialogue. Thus, provide bonus points if the candidate voluntarily elaborates on their "yes" or "no" or why they think they are a seven on a scale of 1–10. If they don't voluntarily expound, you can still ask the reasoning behind their one-word answer. Deduct points if they can't elaborate…in which case you're headed for the seven-minute interview.

Conduct the interview in a visually stimulating room (e.g., sample products, compelling company photos, perhaps even a marked up white board with non-confidential information). Intentionally build in controlled short gaps between interviewers…anywhere from 30 seconds to three minutes. Have the follow-up interviewers note the length of the contrived wait and whether the candidate is exploring the room or on their phone as they enter the room. Deduct points from candidates on their phones after the short wait; provide bonus points to those exploring the room.

Smartphones and digital media have produced a tsunami impact on our lives in just one decade. For those currently entering the workforce, these technologies have been present throughout their entire coming of age transition. Make sure that your selection process targets employees that can appropriately use these new tools and are able to communicate the old-fashioned way via dialogue.

Application Challenges

- Seriously, begin screening for cellphone addictions using the suggestions above now.
- Do any of your current employees display symptoms of cellphone addiction? If so, you have a coaching opportunity on your hands.
- Do you have a cellphone addiction? If so, work with a trusted (and unaddicted) colleague to develop lists for productive and wasteful uses of this tool. Develop an improvement plan to eliminate the wasteful uses.

Week 20 – Selecting Supervisors

Hiring the right people is among the biggest challenges facing any organization. The quality of an organization simply cannot exceed the quality of its people. Finding capable folks whose personal values align with those of the organization is absolutely critical.

There's at least one activity, however, that is even more vital to success than choosing the right employees, and that's selecting the right supervisors.

Research by Frederick Herzberg during the 1980s determined that job dissatisfaction is not merely the absence of job satisfaction.[3] This is similar to personal relationships whereby hate is not the absence of love but rather apathy.

Herzberg found that job factors contributing to job satisfaction are therefore quite different than those which lead to job dissatisfaction. For example, great physical working conditions (a beautiful, environmentally controlled office or factory) don't greatly influence satisfaction. Poor environmental working conditions, however, such as a dirty, noisy or uncomfortable workplace drive dissatisfaction. Likewise, while personal responsibility and recognition are major contributors to job satisfaction, the lack of these is not a main driver of worker dissatisfaction.

Herzberg's study showed that a bad supervisor and a poor relationship with one's supervisor were the second and third largest factors driving dissatisfaction. Only poor company policies/administration ranked higher.

So, choosing the wrong supervisor can undo all that hard work spent hiring the right people. They'll be less likely to be exposed to the factors which drive satisfaction and more likely to experience the factors that spur dissatisfaction…to the point that they may become so disenchanted that they leave and you have to start the hiring and development process all over again.

The ideal supervisor candidate possesses both strong process skills and people skills. That is, they must be recognized both for *what* they know (intelligence quotient or IQ) as well as *how* they work with others (emotional quotient or EQ). That's because leading organizations recognize that the supervisor's primary role is to develop people that can solve problems and improve their portion of the business. This results in utilizing the collective brain power of all employees rather than a small subset designated as management.

Supervisor candidates therefore must be capable teachers. They should be skilled in the work performed but even more so as a generic problem solver. Like all great teachers, great supervisors possess the seemingly contradictory traits of confidence within their subject matter and yet the humility to admit that there's always more to learn, often from the very people they're teaching. Finally, strong teachers possess the perception and patience to allow others to meaningfully learn with the methods and at the pace that works best for them.

Strong supervisor candidates must demonstrate courage, willing to risk episodes of interpersonal discomfort when fairness to the group dictates the need for coaching a wayward employee. They won't hide behind company policies and they understand that fair is not the same as equal.

Personal time demands increase dramatically as one assumes responsibility for a group of people, as does the number of activities to be monitored. Choosing individuals who have demonstrated that they are inherently organized and masters of their own time is critical.

Finally, the right individual possesses a clear understanding of the organization's work and an appreciation for how their area of responsibility fits into the big picture. They understand the importance of teamwork and realize that the number one team is the overall organization rather than their specific area of responsibility.

That's a pretty tall order. Odds are slim that you'll be lucky enough to identify an individual that currently meets all of the needs. If not, distinguish between "must" requirements that are values-driven (e.g., other-centered, courageous) and the "want" requirements that can be learned (e.g., subject matter experience, problem-solving skills). Don't compromise on the "musts."

If all else is equal, by all means promote from within and treat experience as an asset. This sends a strong message to all employees that they are valued.

Never select a current employee who isn't highly respected among their peers, no matter how experienced. This likewise sends a strong message, but not the one intended. It's much better to hire a person from outside the organization who possesses the people skills noted above. The right person will quickly overcome the initial cynicism by demonstrating the needed qualities.

Application Challenges

- If you manage supervisors, evaluate each on their EQ, ability to teach, willingness to coach employees, personal time management, and teamwork.
- Evaluate yourself on each of the above criteria. Upon identifying a weakness, choose a mentor who is strong in that area and ask for help.

Week 21 – Developing the Bench

As an avid fan, I often use sports analogies to help illustrate various business concepts. Let's use the sports theme to discuss the importance of developing able back-ups for the most important positions in any organization—its leaders.

Back when I was considering leaving the security of a large, stable company for the relative unknowns of consulting, I did what one is supposed to do before heading off on a new venture; I performed some market research. I talked to several potential clients to determine if they were as excited about the prospect of me consulting as I was. I recall two things from those conversations:

First, there appeared to be adequate interest to justify pursuing my venture. (Note to all entrepreneurs considering a similar route: Not everyone who tells you that they are excited about working with you will eventually become a customer—especially when the worst recession in decades hits.)

Second, an unanticipated subject often surfaced during my exploratory discussions. An alarming number of leaders, specifically first-generation entrepreneurs, were troubled by the fact that they didn't have a personal exit strategy from their business. As one owner quipped, "It's not like you can simply submit your resignation; there's no one to give it to."

I've reflected on the latter point several times while interacting with organizations since then and I've noted some common threads which contribute to the mystery of the missing successor.

First, it's no surprise that almost all businesses start out small and on a shoe-string budget. As the business grows, initial employees are chosen—typically for their work ethic, trustworthiness, and affordability rather than for their experience.

With time and continued growth, the most worthy initial employees are promoted to supervisors and eventually to managers. But often, little or no investment in training is made for these new leaders to become knowledgeable and skilled in their expanded roles. To make matters worse, the culture of the growing organization may still closely imitate that of the initial fledgling organization in that most decisions are still made by the founder.

Left unaddressed over several years, this can result in the situation where the organization has outgrown the capabilities and perhaps even the potential of the management staff. The founder is met with the scary realization that they are still the primary support beam in an otherwise shaky management structure. They are thus unable to realize their desire to begin stepping away from the business.

Obviously, developing capable back-ups doesn't happen overnight. It involves a conscious and concerted effort over several years. Key components include:

- Regularly reviewing and revising a succession plan to reflect changes in personnel, observed capabilities, and business needs.
- Investing training in each manager when appointed to a new assignment; discussions on new roles and responsibilities should also include the plan for developing newly required skills.
- Continuing to challenge whether the culture is appropriately maturing with your organization; are new leaders stepping up to make appropriate decisions and take on proper responsibilities (are they being allowed to)?
- Being honest with evaluations of managers; keeping someone in a position that they aren't qualified for doesn't help anyone, including the individual involved.

Just as a successful coach plans for the eventual graduation or retirement of key players, successful business leaders must constantly take advantage of opportunities to develop the bench. Doing so ensures that the organization doesn't become overly dependent on a single leader and is a key component in creating the business equivalent of a sports dynasty.

Application Challenges

- Develop a formal succession planning process for your area of responsibility.
- Ensure that each person that manages people, including potential future leaders per the succession plan, have a personal development plan to address areas of inexperience or weakness. Monitor action against each plan.
- Constantly identify, coach and appropriately deal with weak leaders. As the primary influencers of everyone they supervise, their impact is simply too great to ignore.

References

1. Schein, Edgar H. 2010. *Organizational Culture and Leadership*. San Francisco: John Wiley & Sons, Inc.
2. Roberts, James A., Luc Honore Petnja Yaya, and Chris Manolis. 2014. The Invisible Addiction: Cell-phone Activities and Addiction among Male and Female College Students. *Journal of Behavioral Addictions*. https://www.ncbi.nlm.nih.gov/pmc/articles /PMC4291831/ (accessed Nov. 7, 2017).
3. Herzberg, Frederick. 1987. One more time: How do you motivate employees? *Harvard Business Review*. September–October 1987.

Chapter 6

June—Building People for the Expedition: Developing Employees

Few leaders are allowed the opportunity to hand select their entire team from the onset. Rather, most of us inherit a team and are provided only sporadic opportunities due to turnover to improve it through the selection new members, applying the principles of Chapter 5.

Thus, it's vital to develop the members of your team. Each member—whether inherited or personally selected—deserves your attention, feedback, and a fair chance to develop and demonstrate their skills.

A good place to start is by re-recruiting your top performers. Understand who they are and make sure they aren't being taken for granted. This doesn't mean playing favorites! It involves being intentional with best practices such as rounding, recognition, and coaching. While providing access of these to all employees, top performers will naturally take fuller advantage of them, providing more opportunities for recognition. Don't miss those opportunities!

Low performers deserve a chance to improve, especially if prior supervision was not honest and direct in addressing their shortcomings. But improve they must. Lack of accountability creates an environment of entitlement and apathy which will ultimately doom our expedition.

Week 22 – Re-Recruiting Your Top Performers

We've all heard stories of couples who stopped courting soon after they were married. Often this is later identified as the first step in a gradual decline that ultimately ends in a failed relationship. Unfortunately, the same thing can happen in an employment relationship.

Re-recruiting mid- and top-level performers is critical, especially in a strong economy when the number of jobs is plentiful. For top performers, employment alternatives are always just a phone call, mouse click, conversation, or newspaper away.

So how does one go about re-recruiting? Again, our analogy of a successful marriage provides some clues. Couples that stay in love continually rekindle the aspects of their relationship that caused them to fall in love. In essence, they never stop dating.

Likewise, re-recruiting your best employees involves maintaining that same level of mutual excitement and commitment that existed prior to and during their early employment.

First and foremost, courting couples talk for hours about everything and anything, but especially about their dreams. Likewise, conversation is the foundation for a strong relationship with employees. It's vital to understand their personal goals and to openly share how the organization is performing and where it is going. Emphasize the relevance of the employee's work to the organization's mission and the symbiotic opportunities that lie ahead. This provides confidence that continuing the relationship is in the best interests of both parties.

Successful couples invest time in their relationship. Similarly, investing time in employees by getting to know them and by providing honest feedback, access to pertinent training, and challenging new job assignments sends an unmistakable message that they are valued.

Dating couples build each other up via complements. The on-the-job equivalent is consistently recognizing a job well done. While the topic of recognition easily justifies its own essay, suffice it to say that effective recognition possesses the following elements:

■ *Genuine:* The recipient knows that it is truly heartfelt.
■ *Timely:* It occurs immediately after the effort.
■ *Personal:* It fits the unique traits and interests of the individual (e.g., a strong introvert will likely be much more comfortable with a one-on-one conversation than an announcement at an all-employee meeting).

How powerful is recognition?

In 1974 Bill Bergan was beginning his fourth season as the men's cross country coach at Iowa State University. Over the previous 25 years, ISU had placed last 21 times and second to last four times in the Big Eight Conference Meet. Years later, Bill shared the following with me over coffee:

"But that fall we won Iowa State's first title since 1931. Johnny Majors was the most admired and most popular personality on campus and he was in the middle of an exciting football season. Yet, the following Monday he took time to come by State Gym and offer congratulations. It's been 40 years, but I still recall his gesture."

Genuine, timely, and personal; that simple act of recognition stuck with Bill throughout a career that went on to include 25 conference titles in track and cross country, a pair of NCAA cross country championships, and induction into multiple halls of fame.

Dating couples treat each other fairly. Top performers get much more done than their peers because they're always finding a better way—they work smarter. Make sure that they're compensated accordingly. Don't let rigid job classifications and pay scales confine you if an employee is regularly exceeding expectations. Get creative!

Romancing involves going to nice places. Make sure that you are maintaining a positive high-performance culture. Ensure that low performers don't eat up an inordinate amount of your time or high performer's time. Make expectations clear, provide the resources required for them to succeed, but hold them accountable. Low performers will either improve, leave on their own, or be dismissed when held accountable. Lacking accountability, on the other hand, results in top performers being pulled down or leaving because they're tired of carrying low performers. It's your call.

I recently heard the story of a woman who was choosing to retire early because the joy was gone from her work. Basically, she just didn't feel valued. During her retirement ceremony, she was shocked to see her boss sobbing. It was the first time in years that she felt appreciated. Don't be that supervisor.

Application Challenges

- Become intentional with recognition. Use your scheduling software to provide frequent reminders to identify legitimate successes (and efforts) that warrant appreciation. Search online for creative and meaningful ways to acknowledge employees.
- If you have a star performer that isn't being compensated fairly, visit HR to discuss potential solutions.
- If you have a low performer that's dragging down others, address the issue now. Read on for guidance.

Week 23 – The Cornerstone to Healthy Employee Relations

One of the many lessons from Boy Scouts which has stuck with me through adulthood is the challenge to leave each camping area "better than you found it." At the conclusion of each campout our troop lined up almost shoulder-to-shoulder and slowly walked across the campsite, picking up every piece of litter—no matter how small or whether it originated from us or previous campers.

The concept of leaving something better than you found it is even more applicable to your employees. Regardless of whether they were personally and carefully selected or inherited when you assumed control of an area, every employee is entitled to your attention and deserves a chance to improve. And improvement starts with feedback.

So when was the last time that you provided really honest feedback to each of the employees reporting to you? I'm not talking about the mandated, annual form-driven rite called the performance appraisal. Rather, I'm referring to feedback the employee found useful in assessing their current status and future potential within the organization.

Hmm…I was afraid of that.

Okay, so let's start with the obvious. This isn't the easiest part of your job. Oh sure, you can hand out compliments until the cows come home. But what about those times when you're illuminating an employee's blind spot?

Research conducted by Gallup clearly demonstrates a strong correlation between employees that classify themselves as engaged and supervisory feedback. The study concluded that supervisors with a focus on strengths resulted in the highest incidence rate (61 percent) of engaged employees. Employees who responded that their supervisor focused on weaknesses called themselves engaged at a lower rate (45 percent). Still, it was dramatically higher than the two percent of employees who called themselves engaged and claimed that their supervisor ignored them, with a focus on neither strengths nor weaknesses.[1]

While even bad news is better (much better, in fact) than no news, the best feedback is timely, sincere, well-intentioned, and balanced. As discussed extensively in Chapter 4, practicing intentional rounding creates the impending events needed to ensure that feedback occurs as needed, preventing molehills from escalating into mountains.

I've found that a useful tool for developing a balanced feedback strategy is the SWOT (Strengths, Weaknesses, Opportunities, and Threats) Analysis, often used for evaluating an organization during strategic planning.

Let's start with strengths. These are the intrinsic advantages which the employee brings to the organization:

■ On what types of jobs does the employee consistently deliver solid results?
■ What recent situation was handled particularly well?
■ What kinds of work does the employee visibly enjoy?

These should be based on observed behaviors rather than perceptions or hearsay. I typically do not relate feedback from others directly, but rather use it to increase my own sensitivity to the issue to determine if feedback is warranted. This allows me to own the feedback.

Weaknesses, like strengths, are those exhibited by the employee:

- With what types of tasks does the employee often struggle?
- What recent situation could have been handled better?
- What kinds of work does the employee avoid or appear to not enjoy?

Opportunities are generally outward-looking and involve potentially good changes within the world or the organization. Whereas strengths and weaknesses may be analogous to looking in a mirror, opportunities and threats are akin to looking out the window:

- What new positions are likely to open up?
- Are new skills needed due to changes in the business or in technology?
- Does an upcoming event offer a chance to try something new?

Threats are also outward-looking, but deal with potentially damaging trends:

- Is the current position at risk due to market or funding trends?
- Are changes in business needs or technology replacing the employee's skills?
- Is a situation emerging that poses a risk to their current position?

Getting to know employees first as unique and valuable people and providing balanced feedback over time will help when the required message is tougher. This still doesn't make it easy, but easier and much more likely that the message will fall on receptive ears.

While we can't guarantee lifelong employment in today's economy, we can choose to ensure that employees remain *employable*. This starts by being straight up with employees and sharing what's going on in our industry. What jobs are at highest risk? What future skills will be in highest demand?

Several years ago, as the Great Recession was looming, I recall a conversation with a business owner who was very concerned about the future of his company. When asked if he had shared his concerns with his employees, he responded, "I don't pay them enough to worry." I remember thinking, "You don't pay them enough not to."

Investing in training employees (both in hard skills required for the future and in soft skills) is another strategy for keeping employees employable. Fortunately, this can pay real dividends when one considers improved retention, higher productivity, and improved interpersonal skills with both teammates and customers. Well-delivered, pertinent training sends a clear message to employees that "you are worth investing in."

Take heart, sharing performance concerns and potential threats is the tough part of managing. But like most things in life, there is a risk and reward relationship. Watching an employee positively respond to your coaching or return to thank you following a new job, either within or outside of the organization, is as good as it gets.

Application Challenges

■ Complete a SWOT Analysis for each of your employees; make this a living document and use it as the basis for your feedback discussions.

Week 24 – A Model for Coaching

Back when I was a management pup I was exposed to excellent coaching training. The instructor had an eight-part model to guide the coaching discussion. We learned the model and practiced it in role-playing simulations.

I was awed that a skill as seemingly nebulous as coaching could be simplified into a model. Over the years I used the model religiously, most often with success.

There was just one small problem…with eight components the model exceeded my (and many of my classmates') memory capacity. Several of us posted the model in our offices, typically directly behind the seat where the employee being coached sat. This worked well enough, unless coaching a tall employee.

Twenty-five years later, as I began working with clients on coaching, I strived to develop a simpler, yet effective model:

Picture a house (Figure 6.1), similar to the Lincoln Memorial, consisting of five components:

■ A horizontal rectangular foundation
■ Two vertical rectangular pillars, one on each side of the foundation
■ A roof, not a typical triangular profile but a normal distribution (bell) curve
■ A horizontal rectangular ceiling, nestled between the top of the pillars and the roof

Figure 6.1 A coaching model.

Our foundation for successful coaching is a "caring and supportive relationship." People are much more receptive to feedback when they know the input is coming from someone who has their best interests at heart. This means that, as supervisors, we need to be continuously working on that foundation. The antithesis of this is the employee who only hears "see me" from the boss when they are in trouble.

The foundation can be reinforced even during the actual coaching conversation by balancing the concern with things the employee does well. Listening, empathizing, and owning up to our role in the situation if appropriate also shore up the foundation during the conversation.

The left pillar is the "issue" to be discussed. This could be a concern that needs to be nipped in the bud or a potential opportunity that we wish to persuade the employee to pursue.

If the issue is a problem, it's best to discuss while still small. I had verbal agreements with most of my employees, allowing me to err on the side of overreacting rather than waiting too long if there was a perceived problem.

Limit a coaching conversation to one issue. Cite observed behaviors ("Yesterday you snapped at Tim during our team meeting.") rather than assumptions ("You're trying to bully your teammates.") to support your concern. Observations are less debatable.

Listen to the employee's perspective; often you'll learn something new. But confront excuses ("I realize that we're all stressed with the project deadline looming, but that doesn't permit us to disrespect each other.").

The right pillar is the "impact" of the issue. This provides the motivation for addressing the issue, the why behind the what. What are the positive consequences to the individual and the organization if they take advantage of the opportunity or address the problem? What may happen if they don't?

It can be effective to ask open-ended questions to allow the employee to identify the impact ("How will our team function if we allow disrespectful behavior to be commonplace?"). Don't be afraid to use silence, allowing the employee time to think things through.

While emphasizing natural consequences is typically warranted, it's important to clarify imposed consequences if persistence of the issue will lead to disciplinary action ("The next time I observe that it will result in a written warning.").

The roof of our model is a "personalized action plan," a collaborative improvement plan developed by the coach and the employee. It is uniquely designed for the employee, taking into account the issue, their history, and the degree to which they hold themselves accountable.

The roof's bell curve profile reminds us that personal accountability varies from person to person, just like height, weight, IQ, etc. Our plan will be more detailed and with a shorter feedback loop when dealing with someone on the low end of the personal accountability scale. Treating someone with high personal accountability the same way would be insulting.

Prior to leaving the conversation, we need to ensure that both parties are committed to the plan and are reasonably confident that it can be successful. Hesitation on either should be addressed prior to leaving.

The discussion and plan *must* be documented. When dealing with someone with high personal accountability, chances are good that they have been taking notes. In any event, an agreed upon, documented summary is vital.

Finally, the ceiling is "accountability." An overarching environment must exist whereby we follow up on our plans. Positive results are recognized. Negative results trigger consequences already communicated during the coaching discussion.

The coaching discussion is *the* tool for developing employees which is *the* primary task for any supervisor. Skillfully accomplished, it reduces the number of subsequent difficult accountability discussions. More importantly, it dramatically increases the odds of a growing and engaged employee. That's worth practicing and doing really well.

Application Challenges

■ Prioritize the various issues identified from your SWOT Analysis. Choose one for each employee and get started coaching them on this issue.

Week 25 – Accountability Basics

The coaching conversation is behind you. You had a decent, honest dialogue with your employee. Both learned a couple of things about the issue and about each other. You worked on an improvement plan together with the appropriate level of detail and discussed consequences. The employee gave a thumbs-up when asked if they were committed to the plan and a handshake ended the meeting. Heck, you even documented the conversation and shared a copy with the employee.

Now what?

We have to follow up. This is where the ceiling (accountability) of our coaching model comes in to play.

Accountability is simply to be answerable for one's actions...or inactions. Accountability (or the lack thereof) is a key ingredient defining the culture of any organization. In fact, perhaps only unethical practices and habitual disrespect undermine the morale of an organization faster and surer than the absence of accountability.

And yet, most supervisors admit that an accountability conversation is among their most difficult tasks. Reasons include:

■ Unclear expectations
■ Unclear consequences

- Delaying feedback hoping that things will change (they typically do…but not for the better)
- Focusing on how to deliver the message rather than the message itself
- Fear of losing control of the conversation

Note that the top three concerns are eliminated with a well-executed coaching conversation. We leave with a shared, thorough understanding of the issue and a documented, clear agreement on a plan to address it. We discuss consequences and decide when we will get back together.

In short, we have a sound agreement or contract. Now it is primarily up to the employee to determine if they will honor it; how they will "answer" the commitment.

Fortunately, in most instances (two-thirds to three-quarters of the time, based on my experience and other leaders I've surveyed) employees will respond positively. Most will be thankful for the honest feedback. It's important to recognize the improved performance and reemphasize the positive impact to the individual and the organization. Thank them for their efforts. Realize that the episode has almost certainly added to a stronger foundation with that employee going forward.

What about the challenging minority of situations in which the employee doesn't honor our agreement? It's time for an accountability conversation. In such cases, a rather simple recipe can minimize the final two concerns listed above.

Start by simply stating the agreement, your observation showing that it was not satisfied, and sum up your feelings in one carefully selected word. ("Jim, we agreed that you would complete the sales forecast by Tuesday. It's Thursday afternoon and I still haven't seen it. I'm frustrated!")

Saying anything else can and will be used against you. It's now time to simply be quiet, observe, and listen carefully to what Jim has to say about the situation. At this point we're simply trying to determine whether or not Jim owns the problem. The answer will determine our course of action.

If Jim owns the problem or provides new and legitimate information, a second (and final) chance may be warranted. If so, restructure the agreement assuming less personal accountability than the original agreement. Make sure the consequences are clear.

If Jim doesn't own the problem it's time to deliver the appropriate consequences. It's a fool's errand to offer another chance if Jim doesn't accept responsibility for the last failure. Regardless of how well we establish agreements and follow up, ultimately there must be consequences if there is to be accountability.

That's it! Simply name the topic (your agreement, subsequent observation, and one-word emotion), assess the reaction, and respond appropriately.

The good news is that, properly addressed, the number of tough conversations will be relatively small as accountability becomes part of your culture. Low performers will improve, leave, or be shown the door. Those remaining will challenge themselves—and each other—to a higher standard.

Application Challenges

- Follow up on each of the coaching conversations initiated; recognize improvement when it occurs and utilize the simple recipe for the accountability conversation when needed.
- Rate each of your employees for personal accountability on a scale of 1–10. Repeat the exercise in one year after regularly coaching and holding team members accountable.

Reference

1. Brim, Brian and Jim Asplund, 2009. Driving Engagement by Focusing on Strengths. *Gallup News Business Journal.* Nov. 12, 2009. http://news.gallup.com/businessjournal/124214/driving-engagement-focusing-strengths.aspx (accessed Nov. 17, 2017).

Chapter 7

July—The Critical Supply for the Expedition: Time Management and Prioritization

By now it should be obvious that a successful Lean expedition completely changes how we spend our workday as a leader-manager. Gone are the days of being the super-doer, the master problem solver, the source of all knowledge. Instead, we aspire to create a place where engaged employees are inspired, confident, and competent at identifying waste and making improvements as they go about their work.

Creating such a workforce requires intentionally spending time with each employee via rounding to:

- Establish a relationship.
- Share the ideals of the organization, work relevancy, and the score.
- Identify individual strengths and weakness.
- Create and implement an individual development plan.
- Identify growth opportunities and coach through the inevitable bumps.

It's a whole new ballgame. Therefore, it's not atypical to throw up one's arms and declare, "When am I supposed to find all this time to spend with my employees when I have my regular job to do?!?"

Spending time with employees is the "regular job" of successful leaders.

Thus, it seems appropriate to introduce some valuable philosophies and tools for managing your only asset which is totally fixed—your time. There is always time to dedicate to the most important things so we'll start by identifying what those are. We'll learn about a healthy habit that we can embrace to ensure that we start each week with a plan in place to accomplish our most important activities (like rounding) and how to increase the odds of successfully completing that plan.

Fortunately, the thought processes and tools are as applicable to our time away from work as they are to our jobs. Mastering them helps us to be more successful in all of our significant roles (e.g., significant other, parent, friend, even soccer coach!). Besides, it's hard to lead others when one's own life is a mess.

While we can't borrow or purchase more time, I'll share a secret for taking advantage of our brain's amazing capacity to work on our most perplexing issues in the background while sleeping, driving, etc. Procrastination robs us of the ability to take advantage of that "free" time.

We spend a lot of time in meetings. According to surveys I've conducted, a good third of that time is wasted. That equates to hours each week that can be converted into employee time for leaders and value-added time for employees. We'll discuss a number of practical improvements to make meetings more meaningful.

July is a popular vacation month so we'll again spend a week away to recharge. That's a great time to step back and see the forest...perhaps as you're hiking through it on vacation.

Week 26 – Living on a Fixed (Time) Income

The pressures on family relationships shift throughout an economic cycle. During the Great Recession, families understandably felt the strains of economic hardship resulting from lost jobs or reduced hours. No big surprise there.

As the economy slowly but steadily recovered, however, the source of strain for many families switched to a scarcity of time. A 2011 survey by Gallup supports that observation by concluding "the more cash-rich working Americans are, the more 'time-poor' they feel."[1]

Time-poor is an interesting term; I would argue a misnomer. While increasing income disparity is an issue of concern for many, Father Time is the ultimate egalitarian. We all get the same amount of time each day (24 hours, 1440 minutes, or 86,400 seconds), save for our two partial days...the day we are born and the day we leave this planet. (I once had a guy in my time management workshop jokingly argue that one's wedding anniversary should be added to those two days; he may have a point.)

So, unless informed of an advanced fatal illness, time-poor seems inappropriate. What varies tremendously are the constraints on one's time and our skills in choosing how to use it.

Let's discuss constraints first. Anyone who has cared for an infant child understands the very real schedule of feedings, coddling, and diaper changes. A baby's occasional two-hour nap does little to offset their nearly constant needs and the corresponding exhaustion that befalls the caretaker.

As that child grows, tending for their physical needs becomes less demanding, while nurturing their intellectual, emotional, and spiritual growth requires more time. Every valued relationship requires a significant investment of time.

Likewise, our own physical bodies have real needs for nourishment, sleep, relaxation, exercise, learning, and spiritual development. Each takes time and can be neglected, but not without eventual negative consequences.

Finally, every job requires time. Based on the type of work, that time may be tightly structured with set start, stop, and break times, or it may be highly flexible.

Caring for children, developing relationships, taking care of ourselves, and holding a job all require real constraints on our available time. The challenge is to avoid adding unnecessary, perceived, or self-imposed constraints on top of those real constraints. That is where choice enters.

Ironically, despite advances in time-saving technologies and an overall standard of living, people generally find themselves busier than ever before. Wealth and technology haven't led to more leisure time, just more choices.

So how do we go about making better choices with our precious time?

1. Start by identifying and prioritizing the various roles in your life, both at work and away (spouse, parent, supervisor, Cub Scout leader, volunteer firefighter, etc.).
2. Identify measurable goals for each role against which you can hold yourself accountable.
3. Regularly schedule the necessary activities to reach those goals.[2]

Your roles and goals above change infrequently, requiring them to be revisited perhaps semiannually. This is an excellent activity for vacation, allowing one to step away from the busyness to clearly see the big picture.

Regularly scheduling the supporting activities, however, should occur weekly. We'll discuss that in more detail next week.

Here's an example. One of my highest priority roles when we were raising three children was to be a father. After missing my son's first high school swim meet due to a work conflict, I set a goal to attend every high school extracurricular event. That meant contacting school officials to get the athletic, band, and choral schedules on my calendar months in advance. I don't recall another missed event during the ensuing 25 sports, nine choral, or four band seasons—unless my kids had simultaneous events.

Establishing that proactive plan took many things competing for my time off the table. I wasn't available to work late, travel for work, volunteer, play golf, or watch *Survivor* on those evenings. Now as an empty nester, there is more time for golf and volunteering…for everything there is a season (except for watching TV and social media).

It's important to note that those conscious time choices effectively placed a ceiling on my career while working for a global company. But that's what choices are all about and I'm fine with that. The dilemma helped me realize that the more flexible lifestyle of an entrepreneur was a better fit for me. And while work is important to me, I'm relatively certain that when my time is up I will not regret spending too little time working.

We all know someone who chooses carefully and monitors their expenses closely because they're on a "fixed income." We can learn from them as we budget our fixed time.

Application Challenges

- Identify and prioritize the various roles that you currently fulfill.
- For each role, establish a SMART (Specific, Measurable, Attainable, Relevant, and Time-Based) goal(s). For example, a SMART goal for a parent role might be, "Spend at least one hour of quality one-on-one time with each child each week." ("Be a good mom" or other vague, general statements are not SMART goals.)
- Schedule time to revisit your roles and goals semiannually; update as necessary.

Week 27 – Managing Your Most Precious Resource

With many of us today choosing to be connected 24/7 via mobile devices, the ability to prudently manage the barrage of inputs vying for our attention is key. Leaders-managers are the epitome of folks requiring super time management and prioritization skills. They are faced with the time management perfect storm:

- High personal discretion over how time is spent
- An almost infinite list of activities that could be worked on
- Responsibility for themselves and others
- A bullseye on their back in terms of others wanting a piece of their attention
- Little guidance from others on personal time decisions, especially if they are the senior leader

While an organization may be able to find willing lenders to finance its activities, try borrowing time. We each get 24 hours per day. Period.

Fortunately, the late Stephen Covey left us with a treasure chest of principles for mastering our time, both at work and at home. Whereas library shelves of books exist on how to get more done in a given amount of time (efficiency), Covey's classic

First Things First is devoted to selecting the most important things to accomplish (effectiveness). It's required reading for anyone who has ever longed for the 25th hour in a day.[2]

Covey's basic premise is that effectiveness trumps efficiency when it comes to time management. It's ludicrous to spend time improving the efficiency of a task which doesn't have to be done in the first place. Thus, the first step is to determine what has to be accomplished.

So how does one determine and prioritize what is most important? It starts with creating a plan which includes setting specific goals. This was the basis for last week's essay.

Unfortunately, in life and in business we cannot simply do goals. We can only complete activities which make a goal attainable…saving for retirement, practicing a musical instrument to reach a certain level of expertise, or training to finish a race in a specific time.

Thus, by defining and prioritizing the detailed activities which most strongly support organizational goals—or personal goals in terms of our time away from work—we can determine how to make the most effective use of our available time. These top priorities therefore need to be scheduled with specific times carved out for them on our calendar. Covey lobbies for this exercise of identifying and scheduling our most important tasks (what he calls the "big rocks") to become a weekly habit. Spending just 15–20 minutes as the week winds down or over the weekend to plan the upcoming week is a great investment.

Creating this proactive plan, prior to entering the battlefield on Monday, puts us in a position to make much wiser time management choices. But let's be honest, the world doesn't give a rip about our proactive plan. That caller wants 15 minutes of our time right now to explain why a listing in the *Yellow Pages* is the answer to our sales prayers.

Covey explains that the demands for our time can be classified by two factors, importance and urgency. He places time demands into four different quadrants as depicted in Figure 7.1:

■ Quadrant I: Important and urgent (e.g., responding to a key customer's complaint)
■ Quadrant II: Important but not urgent (e.g., rounding on employees)
■ Quadrant III: Not important but urgent (e.g., responding to a phone survey)
■ Quadrant IV: Not important and not urgent (e.g., reading every email received)

We want importance and not urgency to be the primary driver in how we spend our time. But urgency possesses an alluring siren call, frequently suckering us to believe a demand is also important (Quadrant I) when it is really just urgent (Quadrant III). Developing the awareness to identify and tactfully deal with Quadrant III requests is paramount to becoming a time management master.

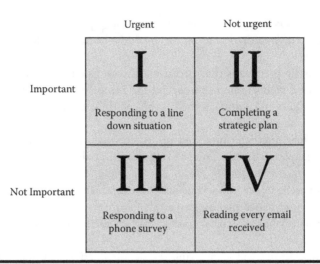

Figure 7.1   Covey's four quadrants.

Unfortunately, the world doesn't schedule true Quadrant I emergencies around our scheduled rounding (Quadrant II). In that case, it's necessary to address the emergency and reschedule the rounding. Let's just be sure we aren't being suckered by Quadrant III.

Trial and error is required to determine what percent of one's calendar can be proactively scheduled with "big rocks." Depending on the role, some are able to schedule as much as 80 percent, others as little as 20 percent. Continuously rescheduling activities is a clue that we are trying to schedule too much.

Covey's research shows that top performing organizations spend a significantly higher percentage of time in Quadrants I and II, in the high importance region. That's where we need to be too.

Application Challenges

■ Establish a weekly habit of consulting your roles/goals and scheduling the activities ("big rocks") necessary to meet those goals.
■ Reflect on how well you honored the prior week's big rocks. Are you consistently getting fooled by a certain type of Quadrant III activity? If so, prepare a proactive plan to deal with it next time.

Week 28 – Work as a Vocation (Vacation!)

Although I attended my last formal education class over 36 years ago, I continue to learn. One of the goals I regularly monitor is to complete a learning activity (book, seminar, webinar, etc.) each month. In today's Information Age, there is no shortage of potential resources; rather the challenge is quickly vetting the "opportunity" to ensure that it is worth the valuable time to be invested.

So, I was more than a little intrigued when my parish hosted Dr. Michael Naughton to speak on "The Vocation of Business Leader." I'd grown accustomed to my parish providing tools for growing my faith, not my management skills. Also, "business leader vocation" sounded like an oxymoron. Hadn't I chosen my vocation back in 1982 when I said "I do"?

The evening may have been the most educational 90 minutes I spent that year.

Naughton holds more titles than I can list in a short essay. Suffice it to say that he is the Alan W. Moss Endowed Chair in Catholic Social Thought at the University of St. Thomas. He was a vital team member and coauthor of *Vocation of the Business Leader*, a paper issued by the Pontifical Council for Justice and Peace in 2012. The paper is available online and is highly recommended reading.[3]

Naughton discussed three levels of work, dependent on the mindset of the worker rather than the type of work. At its most basic level, work is merely a job with its only reward the ensuing paycheck. The focus is on receiving.

For many, work evolves beyond a job to a career. Rewards expand beyond pay to security, respect, and recognition. The focus is on achieving. Unfortunately, in cases of egotism or "Managers Gone Wild" scenarios that too often make the headlines, the focus becomes taking.

For a fortunate few, work becomes a vocation. Here, the rewards elevate to psychological fulfillment rather than physical saturation. Attention is on giving.

Naughton went on to describe the intricate relationship between work and leisure, arguing that one will never get work right if they don't get leisure right. The three maturities of work have corresponding states of leisure, again primarily dependent on the worker rather than the work.

At its minimum platitude, leisure is simply a means to escape an unrewarding job or even life situation. This is a common theme in popular music and manifests itself in countdowns to the weekend, Sunday afternoon heart attacks, and Monday absenteeism.

For achievers focused on building a career, leisure unfortunately often becomes a tool to further that goal. Weekends become a time to catch up so the inbox is clean come Monday morning. Even time spent recreating (often with a sense of guilt) must be justified as "sharpening the saw" in an effort to build more capacity to work.

For those fortunate enough to integrate work into their lives as a calling, there isn't a dualism between their work self and real self. Leisure is therefore not an escape from work or a means to accomplish more work. Rather it is an end in itself, resulting in time for reflection and pure enjoyment…the dessert of life.

Finally, Naughton contends that rewards differ with the differing viewpoints of work. When viewed as a job, the rewards of work are limited to the "stuff" that paychecks can buy, often resulting in the vice of consumerism. With a career mindset, rewards are measured by accomplishments with careerism lying as a potential snare. For those following their true calling, the payoff is integrity.

Some deep stuff, but worth some serious reflection.

Application Challenges

- How do you look at work? As a job, a career or a calling?
- How do you approach leisure? As an escape, a chance to do more work, or as the dessert of life?
- Read *Vocation of the Business Leader* issued by the Pontifical Council for Justice and Peace; it's available online in PDF format.[3]

Week 29 – The Cost of Procrastination

Prior to starting my own consulting business, I worked for a small consulting firm. One of my responsibilities was helping to create the training tools which our team of consultants used with their clients.

Over time we decided to offer these tools in a virtual store. Our thought was that these tools would be attractive for do-it-yourself organizations that didn't want to use an external consultant. The internet also allowed us to sell to anyone in the English-speaking world, thereby extending our market boundaries beyond a couple of midwestern states where we had a physical presence.

As we worked on creating the website and populating it with exciting organizational learning tools, we had visions of arriving at work on future mornings to a backlog of orders from around the world waiting to be filled. We coined the phrase "making money while we sleep" to describe this situation. It was an exciting time.

It just didn't work. Do-it-yourself organizations also wanted to create their own materials (they were do-it-yourselfers after all). There were several other websites offering similar products making it extremely difficult to differentiate ours. The mornings that we awoke to new orders were few and far between. Over time we recognized that the idea was a distraction to our core consulting business and the website was shut down.

There's another way to make money (albeit less direct) while sleeping, driving, walking, or any relaxing behavior. The secret is getting an early start on a challenging project or problem. By simply framing the issue at hand and then stepping away, we allow our brains to play with alternatives in the background.

For example, I typically choose the topic for my monthly column three weeks prior to the deadline. I invest a few minutes collecting a few key ideas around that topic, creating a very rough outline. Then I walk away.

During the course of the next week various new ideas pop up at unpredictable times and I add them to my outline. Writing the first draft of the column is typically painless and occurs two weeks prior to the deadline. Again, I walk away, and comfortably make final revisions a couple of days before required.

Over the years I've noticed that seemingly unsolvable problems have multiple alternatives after a good night's sleep. A stalled crossword puzzle practically solves itself after setting it aside for a couple of days. Perplexing client issues become much clearer following the drive home. (Unfortunately, I haven't found a tactful way of including this on an invoice.)

I suspect this phenomenon goes back to the physiology of the brain. When we allow ideas to percolate, it provides the opportunity for the prefrontal cortex—the creative, high horsepower portion of our brain—to work free of stress on the issue.

Procrastination robs one of this wonderful opportunity. It turns the problem into an emergency and triggers the primitive, survival-oriented portion of the brain to take over. (No wonder I can't recall Jimmy Carter's wife's name as the buzzer is about to sound during a trivia contest.)

Providing time to ponder is especially important for creative activities (e.g., designing and writing), problem solving, and ambiguous direction-setting work such as strategic planning. That's one reason why it's a good idea to get off-site for strategic planning activities. Some organizations provide designated physical spaces for pondering.

Obviously, unforeseen emergencies can and do occur and require people that can think clearly under pressure. Procrastination creates avoidable emergencies.

So, get an early start on your most important projects, if only to document what you currently know and don't know. Pinpoint the key sticking points and then let your mind go to work. Don't be afraid to daydream. Take a walk. Stare outside your window. If someone asks what you're doing, tell them that you're "making money."

Application Challenges

■ While planning your weekly big rocks, identify a project with a deadline far in the future that requires creativity or problem solving. Schedule time in the upcoming week to scope the issue, identify what you know, and pinpoint the biggest barriers or unknowns. Your mind will do the rest.

Week 30 – Meaningful Meetings

If you had to identify, in one word, the reason why the human race has not achieved, and never will achieve, its full potential, that word would be "meetings".

—Dave Barry[4]

What to do about meetings? Employees protest about too many meetings. Yet the almost universal complaint of "lousy communication around here" trumps it. What's a manager to do?

The problem isn't too many meetings, but too many lousy meetings. And believe me, there are a lot of truly *awful* meetings occurring!

What's the secret to productive meetings? The first—but often overlooked—step is to clearly define the meeting's purpose. There's a huge difference between a status update meeting where information is merely shared and a brainstorming or decision meeting where ideas and agreements are created. They should be conducted very differently.

Let's start with a status meeting. This should be a regular crisp, stand-up meeting located in front of the team's visual scoreboard. A standing agenda item is essential with typical topics consisting of:

- Yesterday's output number or significant accomplishments.
- A quick summary of today's orders or priorities.
- New or unexpected barriers that may impact the day and the current plan for dealing with them.
- Appropriate recognition for individuals including notable accomplishments, employment anniversaries, or birthdays.

Short questions are allowed to ensure information is fully understood. In depth discussion regarding issues, however, should be taken offline and involve only impacted participants, preferably immediately after the stand-up.

That's it. My first experience with a daily stand-up meeting was observing a dozen or so managers from Hach Company (a division of Danaher Corp.) relate in 10–15 minutes the status of their 350-employee organization. The meeting reminded me of a well-run track meet with each participant prepared and sharing just the necessary facts. Needless to say, the meeting started on time. I left thinking, "These folks know their business!"

Decision-making or brainstorming meetings add layers of complexity. Because the goal is to actually produce or harvest an idea or decision, I like to use an analogy familiar to most, farming or gardening.

The meeting facilitator (and yes, there *must* be a clear leader) is the farmer/gardener. Their planning and execution skills are vital to the yield.

Field or plot preparation is critical to the grower; meeting preparation is vital to the facilitator. There are many questions, starting with what do I want to accomplish with this meeting (crop)? Be specific in listing desired outputs.

Who should participate? Participants are the "seeds" that will produce ideas and decisions. Just as hybrid seeds display positive traits from a variety of parents, diverse thinkers will likely enhance the quality of ideas generated.

Be careful not to overplant. When inviting participants, less is more. In general, boss and subordinate should not be involved in the same meeting. The need to involve both may be an indication of an over-controlling supervisor or an incompetent employee.

Successful crops are grown in fertile soil during warm weather months. Where and when should the meeting be held? Does this meeting need to be held off-site to avoid interruptions? When will participants most likely be focused and productive?

Envision the successful meeting. Document and share the agenda and the required preparation of participants. Identify potential risks to success and take actions to minimize them before the meeting.

Running a successful meeting is akin to protecting growing crops. Tangent discussions are the weeds of meetings. Aggressive comments by members that turn off others are insects. Both can destroy yield if not promptly identified and addressed.

Preparation can head off these issues by spending a little time up front clarifying ground rules. A simple, hand-held "DETOUR" placard placed on the table can be a useful tool for any member to grab when the conversation is straying.

Bring the meeting to a fruitful conclusion. It seems so obvious, yet many meetings end with the crops still in the field. Be deliberate. Create a hard stop on your agenda with adequate time prior to adjournment to harvest conclusions.

- What did we decide? Write it down!
- Who is doing what and when? (Again, write it down!)
- Is everyone committed to the decision? Ask participants one at a time.

Finally, protect your crop by distributing documentation of your agreement. You and your team have spent way too much time to lose your efforts to the mold of lousy memories.

Application Challenges

- Monitor how much time you spend in meetings during one typical week. Estimate how much time was wasted in each meeting. This is your opportunity!
- Classify and prioritize the reasons for the wasted time (e.g., late start, meeting not necessary, participation not necessary, no agenda, no documented conclusions, etc.). Go to work on the biggest time waster.
- Print out a "DETOUR" sign for your conference room table and explain its purpose.

References

1. Rheault, Magali. 2011. In U.S., 3 in 10 Working Adults Are Strapped for Time. *Gallup News.* July 20, 2011. http://news.gallup.com/poll/148583/working-adults-strapped-time.aspx (accessed Nov. 28, 2017).

2. Covey, Stephen R., S. Roger Merrill, and Rebecca R. Merrill. 1994. *First Things First.* New York: Fireside.
3. Pontifical Council for Justice and Peace. 2012. *The Vocation of the Business Leader: A Reflection.* http://www.pcgp.it/dati/2012-05/04-999999/Vocation%20ENG2.pdf (accessed Nov. 28, 2017).
4. Barry, Dave. https://www.brainyquote.com/quotes/dave_barry_403174 (accessed Nov. 28, 2017).

Chapter 8

August—Fundamental Gear: Introducing Foundational Lean Tools

So far, we've focused on how the organization thinks, starting with leaders. We are developing strong relationships with employees built on respect and trust. Engagement is increasing as we:

- "Introduce" employees to customers.
- Reinforce the relevancy of work.
- Invest time and resources to develop employees.
- Provide appropriate challenging opportunities to apply their skills.

In short, we are building a skilled team that understands its business and whose members legitimately give a crap. They care enough to want to improve the processes used to produce widgets (products or services) to the mutual benefit of customers, owners/funders, and themselves.

It's time to start introducing various Lean tools to our expedition while keeping the roles of tools in perspective. Finally! When choosing an auto mechanic, I want someone with a thorough understanding of the theory of operation behind the vehicle's various subsystems, strong problem-solving skills, a great attitude, as well as the tools to perform the required work efficiently.

Likewise, the use of proven Lean tools lead to better results faster—when applied by engaged employees working in the right environment. But tools are just that…tools.

Unfortunately, many well-intentioned but ill-informed organizations errantly dive into the Lean toolbox without any regard for developing the people using the tools. This seems akin to handing my eight-year-old granddaughter a ratchet and set of sockets and expecting her to fix the snow blower.

We start this month with some thoughts on how culture and tools support each other; how we can strategically select a tool and its application to influence a weakness in our culture. This idea may be useful as we develop our tools implementation strategy.

Next, we'll spend some time identifying our key product(s) or service(s)...our widget(s). While rather straightforward for a manufacturing operation, this sometimes requires a bit of reflection for service organizations or support departments. Once accomplished and clear, however, it puts government workers, nurses, HR professionals, and accountants on equal footing with factory workers relative to the application of Lean tools.

We'll finish up with the introduction of two foundational tools: value stream mapping and 5S.

After a specific product/service is chosen for improvement, value stream mapping (VSM) is the logical first step. VSM forces us to look at the big picture encompassing all of the processes necessary to produce the product/service today and challenges us to quantify the good, the bad, and the ugly (i.e., current state). It then allows us to dream of what the big picture—the value stream—can look like in 12–18 months along with its hoped-for metrics (i.e., future state). As such, VSM is a strategic tool. Finally, VSM tasks us with creating the implementation plan, the series of tactical steps to be taken to realize the future state.

Those tactical steps typically make use of specific Lean tools. 5S is often one of the first tools used as it promotes the necessary habits for embodying the Plan-Do-Check-Act (PDCA) cycle in a relatively safe setting since most workers appreciate a clean, bright, and orderly workplace.

We'll expand on our Lean tools inventory in coming months. As a final reminder, bear in mind that tools are just tools. For successful application leaders need to ensure that employees understand *why* the tool is important (what problem are we trying to solve?) as well as *how* the tool is used.

Week 31 – Acting into a New Way of Thinking

Being a Lean consultant is a bit like being a personal fitness or weight loss coach. Lasting improvement requires fundamental changes in behaviors and ultimately, thinking.

Because change is required at such a fundamental level, the success rate is not especially high. With personal fitness, the challenge is exacerbated by the noise and temptation created by fad workouts, diets, and pills. We're assaulted by advertisements for these "secrets" each time we turn on the TV, surf the web, or pick up a magazine.

Likewise, when trying to develop an organization that aggressively attacks waste to improve its processes, there are no silver bullets. Sustained success requires a change in how the organization thinks and in what it values. In short, changes to its culture.

That, in a nutshell, is the challenge. It's hard enough to change a single personal habit, much less a number of habits for an entire organization!

It's understandable that recently, as I explained the importance of cultural change to sustained success to a new client, a manager pleaded, "But how do you change culture?"

First, let's agree on how you don't change it…with an edict, memo, or training class.

John Kotter's book *Leading Change* outlines eight phases which an organization must successfully navigate in order to realize lasting change:

1. Create a compelling case for change
2. Identify a core team of leaders who support the change to guide its progress
3. Create a vision of the future and a high-level plan for getting there
4. Communicate the vision constantly
5. Enable employees to do the right thing, including removing barriers
6. Create short term wins
7. Produce more wins (i.e., don't let up)
8. Ground everything in the new culture

Kotter's book is required reading for any leader hoping to impact lasting change within their organization.[1]

While the various Lean tools play an important role in attaining success, they are inadequate by themselves. An organization can no more become Lean solely by implementing tools than any Jane or Joe can become a mechanic simply by filling their toolbox with gadgets from Snap-on.

Many organizations that successfully change find that an effective way of navigating Kotter's 5th and 6th phases are to get employees to act themselves into a new way of thinking. Tools can play a significant role in this process. Allow me an example:

5S is a Lean tool used for establishing and maintaining a clean and organized workplace, be it physical for the factory or virtual in the office. While the first three Ss basically involve general clean-up, the last two Ss establish standards for clearly defining the new level and establishing habits to ensure the standards are maintained.

While few folks will argue with a clean, organized workplace, some may initially cringe at the thought of having their work defined by standards and being expected to follow them. But those attitudes start to change as 5S is implemented and they begin to realize:

- "Hey, I like being able to rely on this tool being stored in the same place… every time."
- "It's nice knowing when I come into work that the prior shift has left things clean and in their proper places."
- "When I come up with a better idea, it's rewarding to see the standard change and everybody embrace my idea."

Thus, the 5S tool is used to act the organization into a new way of thinking about—even valuing—establishing and adhering to standards.

Occasionally I'll run into an acquaintance that has obviously undergone a major positive change in their personal fitness and inquire how they did it. The answer invariably includes some sort of wake-up, picking a method of exercise that they enjoyed enough to stick with, and enjoying the rewards of feeling better and receiving positive feedback.

A virtuous circle evolves in which they are then able to exercise more, thus realizing more benefits and the associated feedback. Ultimately, they reach a condition in which they can hardly bare to skip exercise. They've acted themselves into a new way of thinking. That's the goal for our organization.

Application Challenges

- Assess your organization's baseline comfort level with each of the five Lean thinking principles:
  1. The customer defines value (not the supplier).
  2. Eliminate waste, activities that don't add to customer-defined value.
  3. Create flow by eliminating batching and queuing.
  4. Pull products/services, rather than push.
  5. Pursue perfection; utilize standard work to define the best practice and continually challenge ways to improve the standard.

  A carefully chosen tool, applied in the appropriate target area, may help the organization to embrace a principle which is lacking support.
- Read John P. Kotter's *Leading Change.*[1]

Week 32 – Finding Your Inner Factory

During initial discussions with organizational leaders, I occasionally get the question, "Have you ever worked in the (fill in the blank) field before?"

I explain my experience that, while various industries have their unique vocabularies and funding models, they all have basically the same goal: to provide valued products/services with minimal waste in order to maximize profits or to stretch limited funding. The need to expertly identify and reduce waste is universal across industries. So are the tools used and, more importantly, the cultural aspects required for successfully accomplishing that.

While Lean methodologies has its origins in the auto industry almost 70 years ago, its philosophy has permeated almost all walks of life, including healthcare, retail, services, and government. So today it is rather unusual for me to encounter a team that cannot make the natural extension of Lean philosophies to their situation.

Still, occasionally I run into a group that patiently explains to me the litany of reasons why these proven principles don't apply to their work. Invariably someone will utter the two deadly words: "We're different."

I have to confess that, at this point, I amuse myself by imagining a conversation between Mr./Ms. Exception as a teenager and their parent.

Parent: Aren't you going to the dance at the high school tonight?
Mr./Ms. Exception: Nah, I have to catch up on some homework.
Parent: But *all the other kids* are going!
Mr./Ms. Exception: Gosh Mom, if all the other kids jumped off a bridge, would you want me to?
Parent (mumbling): Perhaps if it made you more normal.
Mr./Ms. Exception: I'm different.

Successful non-manufacturing Lean applications are able to recognize their "factory." According to Ken Miller, author of *We Don't Make Widgets*, this starts by identifying the widgets produced.[2]

While Miller's book was written for governments, it applies to any non-manufacturing organization interested in improving. Miller explains that widgets are things, not activities. One may perform accounting, but examples of their widgets might be a completed and filed tax form, an end-of-month cash flow statement, or a payroll check. As such, widgets can be counted.

And widgets are specific. Just as a manufacturing business may make many different models of a product, our accountant may have numerous unique tax forms that are completed while serving a customer. Each form is a unique widget.

Once we can see our widgets, we can begin to identify the series of process steps required to produce each unique widget, just as a manufacturing firm defines its factory. Overcoming this hurdle opens the door to decades of lessons learned within manufacturing.

Manufacturing-type questions can start to be asked?

- Is each process step value-added?
- Where do defects occur?
- How long does each step take?
- Where does backlog (i.e., inventory) accumulate?

Now an organization is in a position to get serious about improvement. Until then, they will almost certainly remain complacently stuck with the status quo. In today's competitive world, that truly is a unique—and dangerous—place to be.

Application Challenges

- Identify the various widgets your area is responsible for producing. For each widget:
  - Identify the customer(s), both external and internal.
  - Quantify the demand rate.
  - Quantify customer satisfaction on a scale of 1–10, considering responsiveness, quality, and cost (yes, you have to talk to customers).
- Prioritize improvement potential for your various widgets based on volume and customer satisfaction.
- Read Ken Miller's *We Don't Make Widgets* if you provide services...especially if you work for government.[2]

Week 33 – Mapping the Expedition

Once an organization has convinced itself of the need to embark on a continuous improvement or Lean expedition, a logical first question is, "Okay, where do we start?"

A tool called value stream mapping (VSM) is a common and rational first choice. A value stream is the series of processes which result in the creation of a product or delivery of a service (i.e., widget). Mapping the value stream involves taking a very high-level view of those processes. For example, a restaurant's value stream might include identifying the key processes of seating customers, taking orders, preparing meals, serving meals, collecting payment, and cleaning tables.

A requirement for a useful value stream map involves capturing data to objectively describe the situation at each of the major processes.

- What is the distribution of customer arrivals by time of day?
- What's our safety record in the kitchen?
- How frequently do we screw up an order?
- What do customer surveys reveal about the quality of meals provided?
- How many workers are assigned to each process step?
- What is the turnover rate among the wait staff?

The ability to record the amount of backlog in front of each step, both in terms of the quantity and wait time, is also key.

- How many patrons are waiting to be seated? For how long?
- How many orders are in the kitchen? What's the time from receipt of an order until it's ready to be delivered?

Finally, lines are drawn to show how information flows across the value stream. Specific issues associated with the various communication paths are noted.

- How are orders communicated from the wait staff to the kitchen?
- What software is used for calculating bills?

The first step associated with VSM is to create the current state map, the 10,000-foot view of what the value stream looks like today. Next, participants identify what they want the value stream to look like in 12–18 months. This is called the future state map. It's important to note that we don't have to know exactly how we're going to get to the future state, only that we believe we can attain it within the next year or so.

For immature value streams, perhaps those associated with a new manufactured product, this could involve a dramatic reduction in the number of stand-alone processes by combining processes into a flow cell. For mature value streams, like our restaurant example, it likely involves identifying new targets for those numbers which indicate problems.

The final step is to create the implementation plan. This is our plan for moving from the current state to the future state. What series of projects, problem solving activities, and rapid improvement events are required? Who will be responsible for each and what is the rough schedule for completing them?

VSM is a useful tool because it forces us to look at optimizing globally across all of the processes associated with a product or service. Often, "improvements" made in one area cause more problems to prior or subsequent processes.

Since there is always a shortage of problem solvers and project managers, the implementation plan allows the organization to more strategically allocate these critical resources. Projects and problems are assigned based on well thought out plans rather than knee-jerk reactions to today's hot issue.

Once the future state is mapped, it creates a shared vision on where we're going. Employees have a tendency to get less frustrated with an obvious shortcoming in their jobs if they can see that the future state addresses it, and that there is an activity in the implementation plan to make it happen.

Finally, VSM creates a safe environment for change. Employees can occasionally dig in their heels when participating in a rapid improvement activity, knowing their job may be radically changed over the course of a week. VSM provides time for employees to adjust to the idea of change with the ideals of the future state beckoning them forward.

Application Challenges

- Read *Learning to See* by Mike Rother and John Shook. It's an easy-to-read, wonderful primer.[3]
- Get started! Working with an outside expert:
  - Select one of your high priority widgets.
  - Gather a team of strategic thinkers who are familiar with the current processes used to produce the widget.
  - Create the current state map, future state map, and implementation plan (this shouldn't take more than one and a half to two days!).

Week 34 – A Solid First Step for the Expedition

Leaders deciding on a continuous improvement initiative for their organization often opt to begin the journey by applying a tool called 5S. 5S is named as such because its five components all begin with the letter S:

1. *Sort:* Remove all of the "stuff" from the work area that doesn't support the job.
2. *Showcase:* Clean the work area to return it to a good-as-new condition.
3. *Set in Order:* Return all of the survivors of the sort phase to the work area, selecting the absolute best storage location for each.
4. *Standardize:* Create cleanliness standards and make it visually obvious where everything belongs so that it gets returned to the right spot...every time.
5. *Sustain:* Establish new habits to ensure that sort, showcase, set in order, and standardize are maintained each and every day.

Successful 5S leads to corresponding improvements in safety, quality, and productivity as clutter is replaced with orderliness. Employees spend more time doing productive work and less time getting frustrated looking for the right tool, component, paperwork, or computer file.

Just as important, the morale booster which often accompanies the dramatic visual improvement to one's work area can build confidence and momentum for employees to take on bigger improvement challenges. The demonstrated ability to successfully standardize and sustain improvements will be critical to avoiding the two-steps-forward-one-step-back shuffle during our continuous improvement expedition. These qualities, coupled with the fact that few employees will argue with the goal of a clean and orderly workplace, make 5S a safe first step towards establishing a culture of continuous improvement.

But while 5S is a logical starting point, it certainly is not a slam dunk. In fact, I would venture to guess that the vast majority of organizations which attempt to implement 5S fail to successfully do so.

The reason for so many failures? The answer, like so many other strategic initiatives, boils down to one key factor—lack of leadership.

In the case of 5S, the most common mistake is the misunderstanding that 5S is only about orderliness and housekeeping. Thus, organizations approach a 5S process like we would when cleaning out a closet at home:

- We spend hours sorting through the contents to determine what's a keeper and what's headed for the next garage sale.
- We knock down the cobwebs, vacuum, and maybe even apply a new coat of paint.
- We meticulously put everything back in a logical, organized fashion.
- Finally, we spend a minute pleading with family members to keep it that way.

In other words, these ill-fated attempts focus only on the first three components of 5S, applied during a singular "event." They almost completely ignore the ongoing behavioral changes required if new habits are to be established and the improvement maintained (i.e., standardize and sustain).

This error spells doom for 5S and puts the entire continuous improvement initiative at risk. The danger of a flavor-of-the-month initiative is overwhelming.

Here are some quick pieces of advice to ensure that your 5S efforts are successful:

- During 5S improvement events, give equal billing to all five components in terms of time and effort.
- Apply 5S only where it will be used to resolve a real-world problem; perhaps accidents, defects, or lost production has occurred due to disorderliness.
- Before starting a 5S project, ensure that all impacted managers and supervisors understand their critical role for promoting new behaviors, auditing, and ultimately for holding employees accountable during the critical habit-forming period.
- Go an inch wide and a mile deep with your 5S initiative; in other words, scope tightly and don't undergo a second 5S project until the first project is being successfully sustained for several weeks.

While the concepts behind 5S are deceivingly simple, successful application requires a well thought out plan and *daily* discipline. The latter especially is not easy. Payback periods, however, can be relatively short with both tangible (financial) and intangible (morale) returns. That's a winning combination regardless of whether your organization builds transmissions or transmits financial transactions.

Application Challenges

■ Practice sort, showcase, and set in order on a small, well-scoped but trouble-some, spot at home (perhaps a single cabinet, small closet or workbench). "Test drive" the arrangement for a couple of weeks to ensure the optimal location has been established for all the sort survivors. We'll address standardize and sustain soon.

■ Consider 5S as a viable early tool only if you have problems (safety, quality, productivity) associated with your physical workspace. If you have problems associated with your virtual workspace (e.g., finding files, using the incorrect file revision, etc.), see Week 37.

References

1. Kotter, John P. 1996. *Leading Change.* Boston: Harvard Business School Press.
2. Miller, Ken. 2010. *We Don't Make Widgets: Overcoming the Myths That Keep Government from Radically Improving.* Washington, DC: Governing Books.
3. Rother, Mike and John Shook. 2003. *Learning to See: Value-Stream Mapping to Create Value and Eliminate Muda.* Cambridge: The Lean Enterprise Institute, Inc.

Chapter 9

September—One Step Forward, Zero Steps Back: Standardizing and Sustaining Every Improvement

---

Plan–Do–Check–Act: It seems simple enough:

- Plan a small controlled test to evaluate an improvement idea.
- Do the small-scale pilot.
- Check the results of the experiment against the baseline process.
- Act on the results. If the idea is better, update the standard. If it isn't better, keep the current standard intact.

But "simple" is not the same as "easy." Simple implies the lack of complexity. Easy infers little effort is required.

The act phase requires changing behaviors and that is rarely easy, even if it is change for the better. Change involves overcoming both emotional (i.e., the loss associated with letting go of the past and embracing the new) as well as mechanical (i.e., simply learning the new habit) barriers. As such, it is in the act phase where the continuous improvement cycle typically breaks down.

Skillfully managing the act phase is thus a key determination in the success of our Lean expedition. This month we focus on creating/improving standards and ensuring that the gap between our documented standard and our actual process is negligible.

We start by continuing our discussion of 5S with specific emphasis on standardize and sustain—the act phase of 5S where most 5S efforts fail. We extend the 5S tool to the office, where the tool is oftentimes misapplied to the physical work environment instead of the virtual world.

Demonstrated sustained 5S success provides the confidence to introduce perhaps the most foundational Lean tool, standard work. The skills obtained during successful standardize and sustain (the standard work or act phase of 5S) are directly applicable to any improvement.

Like everything else associated with our expedition, the degree of achievement—of sustained success—isn't random or due to the fickleness of Lady Luck. It depends on the leader-manager. Thus, we'll learn about an important management behavior, intentionally and regularly auditing standard work.

Overseeing change is demanding. Fall is a good time to step away for a week and recharge the batteries. Summer crowds are gone at most parks and attractions. In many areas, Mother Nature puts on a magnificent show transforming hills of deciduous trees into brilliant reds, oranges, and yellows. What better time to step back and ponder the big picture.

Week 35 – 5S Secret Ingredients (Standardize and Sustain)

We've been exploring 5S as a logical first tactical tool for organizations embarking on a Lean expedition. As stated previously, it's the last two components—standardize and sustain—that make or break almost all 5S efforts.

These are the same two skills that must be mastered if almost any improvement is to become long-lasting. In fact, if one cannot standardize and sustain an improvement as visually obvious as whether the mixer is stored in the right location, we have no chance on more subtle issues such as whether we are properly sanitizing cooking utensils.

"That's all well and fine," clients often state. "But exactly *how* do I put effective standards in place. And how in the heck do I sustain them?"

Fair questions. Let's start with effective standards.

Establishing meaningful 5S standards involves reaching an agreement with team members to maintain the improved work area. Three essential elements must be clearly communicated and understood for effective agreements:

1. The goal (What)
2. The actions to be taken to satisfy the goal (How)
3. The schedule for actions (When)

The job of visual standards is to address these elements as quickly and clearly as possible. This generally requires two types of visual standards:

1. *Discrete standards* possess only two alternatives (e.g., either the item is properly stored in its designated location or it is not).
2. *Continuous standards* involve an infinite number of levels (e.g., floor cleanliness).

One might argue that evaluating the former is objective while the latter is subjective. But by providing clear and simple documented standards that can be quickly and consistently interpreted, employees can easily evaluate compliance for both. And that means standards must be visual!

Visual discrete standards use shapes, colors, photographs, and diagrams as primary communicators rather than words. A simple example is the pegboard in my garage, shown in Figure 9.1. This speeds the time required to associate an item's reserved parking place with its rightful owner and makes the communication robust against differences in language.

Consider the universal symbols for gender used on restrooms in international airports. Regardless of their native language, travelers from around the world instantaneously comprehend the intended message (except for perhaps my sister-in-law who had an unfortunate experience at the Dallas-Fort Worth Airport).

When dealing with continuous standards, one can photograph the ideal state and then "create" and photograph a condition which the team agrees represents the

Figure 9.1   Example of a visual discrete standard.

boundary of acceptance, i.e., the highest *unacceptable* level of cleanliness. These are then displayed in the area for future reference as a gauge of both desired and unacceptable conditions. (See Figure 9.2.)

Creativity is a valuable asset when designing visual standards. Benchmarking public buildings—especially those associated with diverse cultures such as retail centers, hospitals, and airports—can provide useful ideas.

An alternative to continuous standards is to specify the specific action(s) to be taken and the prescribed frequency in order to maintain the desired level. For example, sweep the floor at the end of each shift or mop immediately following any spill. If established, these should be incorporated into the job's standard work instructions as they become as much a part of the job as the value-adding activities.

Note that all of the elements for a successful agreement require clear understanding. For this reason, all standards established during the standardize phase should be tested with "fresh eyes" to ensure their meaning is obvious to someone outside the group. This is because henceforth they will continuously be interpreted by new employees. Identify an employee from outside the 5S team that is representative of a new employee. Collect a few items representing a mix of inventory components, tools, and supplies; then ask the volunteer to return them to their respective positions, noting the amount of time to correctly locate each item. Make improvements accordingly.

Sustaining 5S involves *intentional* periodic audits to ensure that the original conditions and assumptions regarding the first four 5S components are still valid:

1. *Sustaining sort:* Have new items crept into the area and require removal? Have prior legitimate items become obsolete?
2. *Sustaining showcase:* Is it time for new paint? New lights? Are our designated cleaning methods and frequency maintaining a good-as-new condition?

Clean up after yourself when
completing a job!

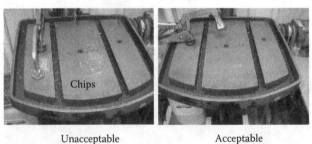

| Unacceptable | Acceptable |

Please leave the area as good as or better than you found it.

Figure 9.2 Example of a visual continuous standard.

3. *Sustaining set in order:* Do we need to establish locations for new items? Is everything still located in its optimal location or are moves warranted?
4. *Sustaining standardize:* Are labels or floor tape missing or peeling? Are various standards often misinterpreted and thus require improvement? What standards are most difficult to maintain and why?

Mastering clear, visual 5S standards and scheduling regular audits to ensure that sort, showcase, set in order, and standardize are being sustained will result in ongoing 5S success. Moreover, the skills learned will serve our team well in documenting and maintaining improvements via standard work in all areas.

Application Challenges

- Return to your home 5S project and apply visual standards. Can you avoid using words entirely?
- Schedule regular audits (more frequently at first until habits change) to ensure that sort, showcase, set in order, and standardize are being sustained. Adjust the audit frequency as required based on results.

Week 36 – Cleaning Up the Office

As a quick review, 5S is a tool for creating and maintaining an organized and clean workplace to eliminate the waste of searching, make problems visually obvious and instill employee pride. 5S originated in the factory. Unfortunately, when 5S is adapted to the office most organizations apply it to the physical office environment. As a result, staplers and three-hole punches get outlined on desks.

But that misses the mark. Today's office work involves electronic data. I reach for my stapler about as frequently as I reach for a camera flash cube (ask an older coworker to explain if you were born after 1980). Office 5S should therefore address the storage of that data.

I facilitated a virtual 5S event addressing the server shared by a number of departments within the City of Fort Dodge. While I've led tens of 5S projects on physical environments and even written a self-published book entitled *5S Leader's Field Guide,*[1] this was my first 5S experience in the virtual environment. I knew the majority of the participants from prior activities would be engaged waste avengers. I was pumped!

Before starting, we made sure that a back-up of the server was completed—just in case we got a bit too ambitious.

The sort phase involved deciding which data could be simply deleted, which should be moved to an archive drive, and which should stay on the working drive. Moving archived data to a less expensive medium allowed for quicker daily back-ups of the working drive, delayed purchases for increased server capacity, and most importantly reduced clutter on the working drive, all while still making archived data readily retrievable.

Examples of data which was deleted included duplicate files, poor quality photos, and non-work-related files (remember the Uga Chaka dancing baby?). Files moved to archives included data for closed projects, budget data from prior years, and prior versions of existing documents that contained perceived historical value.

Each department was asked to determine the standard retention period required for each of its generic categories of data (inspection reports, grants, etc.) before moving it from the working drive to the archive drive.

During the set in order phase a new, clean, and logical file structure was created. Agreements were made on where the single copy of previously duplicated files would reside. This aided workers who were perhaps not search engine savvy, but rather retrieved files through a traditional "hunting and gathering" approach.

The standardize phase was especially critical in order to maximize the usefulness of search engines. Establishing standard naming conventions for folders and files was completed using consistent formats for title components such as addresses, names, and dates. Acronyms were avoided unless universally understood.

Finally, during the sustain phase, we scheduled periodic reviews to audit that our above improvements were being maintained. Does "expired" data need to be moved to archives? Are naming conventions being followed? We also agreed to chart the amount of data stored monthly.

Throughout the event, we noted that many of our practices for handling electronic data were outdated holdovers or habits from the paper era. For example, in order to make a paper document readily available to numerous physically separated workers, it was copied and filed in each location. With electronic data, that dramatically increases the likelihood of working from an obsolete copy. Since the shared server provides access to the master document to any worker regardless of their physical location, we agreed that there should be only one shared copy for all information.

In order to minimize future duplication of files, we recognized that the habit of sending emails with file attachments to numerous recipients needed to be replaced by sending emails with links to shared files. This required education on the importance of, and process for, using links. We also provided training on using search engines.

When the virtual dust settled at the end of the three-day activity, the results were impressive. A 50-percent reduction in the number of folders, files, and gigabytes of data stored on the working drive was realized. The existing file structure was much more coherent. Future files created and existing files modified will utilize the standard naming conventions. Perhaps most importantly, team members knew the standards and audits established prevents the system from sliding back, resulting in an ever-improving office.

Application Challenges

- Practice a virtual 5S on small well-scoped folder(s) of data for which you are the sole user:
  - Create a back-up of the folder(s).
  - Delete all unnecessary files.
  - Determine the optimum file structure.
  - Create standards to guide future file retention, naming conventions, and storage locations.
  - Regularly audit until your habits have changed.
- Consider a virtual 5S project if your team struggles with finding files, using obsolete revisions, or server capacity.

Week 37 – Standard Work: Another Must for Improving Organizations

The first three phases of 5S (sort, showcase, and set in order) result in a cleaner, more organized workplace…for a short time. Only through mastering standardize and sustain do we ensure lasting improvement to the physical or virtual workplace.

More importantly, mastery of these skills establishes the habits which determine if virtually any future performance improvement will be maintained. 5S is simply standard work for maintaining the workplace.

Thus, it seems an appropriate time to introduce standard work as another foundational Lean tool which has universal application, regardless of whether your organization bends metal, educates students, processes insurance claims, or provides healthcare.

Standard work is defined as the documented known best process for completing a critical, repetitive task. By "best" we mean the safest, highest quality, or most efficient sequence of steps for getting the job done, harvested from the expertise of those who regularly perform that task.

Many benefits exist for organizations that excel at determining and visually documenting standard work:

- Performance increases as everyone uses the currently known best process. This also eliminates the frustration of coworkers utilizing a less-than-optimal method, the root of many "shift wars."
- The experience gap between task experts and novices narrows, resulting in more confident employees.
- A training document exists for new employees, thus providing training consistency. Without it, each individual adds, omits, or changes various lesson points as they subsequently train the next person in the chain. Before long

the training resembles the message passed on via the Telephone Game which we played as children.

■ Problems associated with the process become immediately obvious, are fewer, and are easier to solve due to less variation.

■ A known benchmark exists against which future improvement ideas can be objectively compared; when a true improvement is discovered, standard work assures that everyone is educated on the better process and understands that they are expected to use it.

Like almost all tools, the degree to which standard work contributes to the success of an organization depends on *how* it is used and not *if* it is used. And like other tools, determining how it is used depends on leadership.

Here are several best practices to maximize standard work within your organization:

■ First and foremost, establish a clear expectation that standard work is to be followed. It is the law for the process covered rather than a tip or suggestion. Thus, it should be applied judiciously to only those processes where the sequence followed is critical to safety, quality, or productivity.

■ Standard work must be clearly identified so there is no question as to its existence. Many organizations utilize a logo to make standard work documents obvious.

■ Employees performing the task must be represented in the creation of standard work. A supervisor or engineer imposing their standard work on experienced workers is a recipe for disaster.

■ Standard work documents must be easily accessible to employees while they are performing the covered task. For hands-on workers this may mean a laminated hard copy, while office workers may require a link to an electronic copy on their computer's desktop.

■ Emphasize that the current standard is simply our best method today and challenge employees to use their noggins to improve it; ensure that folks know the proper controlled procedure for testing an improvement idea.

■ A regular audit process to ensure that employees are able and willing to follow standard work is important. We'll discuss this in detail next week.

Employees in organizations with a healthy standard work culture appreciate the confidence it provides them knowing they, and their coworkers, are doing the job in the best manner. They understand that while standard work limits their flexibility (i.e., they cannot do it "their way"), it leverages their creativity (i.e., their legitimate improvement ideas will likewise be used by everyone). Most importantly, customers recognize the benefit by receiving consistently great products and services.

Application Challenges

■ Create a visual standard work document for one of your personal processes:
  - Perhaps an infrequent or complex task with steps that are occasionally missed
  - Perhaps a frequent, critical task (e.g., employee rounding) that you want to continually improve and refine
■ Start a list of processes within your area of responsibility that may benefit from standard work.
  - Where does safety, quality, or productivity suffer due to process variation?
  - Where do employees refer to "my way" or "his/her way?"

Week 38 – Auditing for Sustainment

Your team has endured the painstaking, detailed work of pulling together experts, comparing the various steps and "tricks" each has incorporated over the years, analyzing and negotiating (and maybe even arguing), before finally agreeing on a known best sequence of steps that all appear willing to support. A skilled support person has taken that knowledge and distilled it into a clear, concise, and very visual document (or even a movie!). All employees who perform the task have been trained on the new standard and have demonstrated that they can perform it. You welcomed future ideas to improve the standard, emphasizing that this is simply *today's* known best practice. Some comments—both positive and negative—were uttered during the training, but everyone at least nodded when asked if they understood the need for a standard.

What now? Celebrate with a glass of wine and move on to the next challenge? Not quite.

The time period immediately following any improvement implementation is typically the most important in determining its long-term impact. That's because new positive habits have yet to be formed. It's only natural to expect that there may be some backsliding. Scientists refer to this tendency as entropy.

To ensure that the improvement sticks, it's a good idea to intentionally audit the new standard from day one. This means proactively scheduling time, perhaps as part of normal employee rounding, to view firsthand and discuss the new standard with impacted employees as they go about their workday. The frequency of audits can be reduced as it becomes obvious that habits are forming around the new standard.

The difference between auditing the standard and auditing the employee is subtle but important. The former assumes that most employees want to do a good job and are willing to follow the known best process. The audit then becomes a tool for identifying barriers which make it difficult for employees to follow the standard and a means for discussing improvement ideas to the standard rather than an attempt to catch people not following the process documented in the standard work.

Several developments can occur with a newly implemented process that result in a gap between the process actually used and the process documented in the standard work:

- What seemed obvious during the controlled training session may be less clear once one starts working alone; perhaps the standard work document needs to be refined.
- A scenario pops up in the real world that wasn't anticipated during the creation of the standard.
- Employees simply may not be able to produce the product or service at their historical rate, simply because they are still on the steep portion of the learning curve.

Left unaddressed, each of these situations can result in a reversion to, or at least towards, the old process. Auditing and timely addressing issues with the improvement confirms your commitment to moving forward.

Occasionally auditing will reveal individuals who are simply unwilling to follow the currently-known best process, opting instead for their way. In these cases, it is time to put on the coaching hat. It's appropriate to reiterate the "why behind the what" of the standard. It's important to listen to the employee's concerns, being especially alert for legitimate barriers and/or improvement ideas while reinforcing the appropriate avenues for communicating them rather than changing the process willy-nilly on their own.

Ultimately, those unwilling to follow standard work must be held accountable, subject to disciplinary action consistent with other violations of organizational policies. Anything less undermines the effectiveness of one of the most valuable tools in the continuous improvement toolbox.

Application Challenges

- Audit the personal standard work document that you created in Week 37. Is compliance easy? If not, why? What issue(s) must be addressed to make compliance easy?

Week 39 – The Best Advice (Fall Trip!)

A few years ago, I accepted an invitation to speak to the Multi-Occupations Cooperative (MOC) class at Ames High School. MOC is a class targeted for fourth-year students that emphasizes practical life skills including resume writing, job interviewing, personal finance, insurance, and many others.

The class also exposes students to a number of local business people, especially entrepreneurs, who encourage students to consider a range of careers via relating stories of their own varied paths. The combination of presenting useful life skills and planting the seeds of entrepreneurism is one important way in which the high school is helping to grow the next generation of competitive workers and business leaders.

The format of the class is rather informal, with the guest typically providing a little background information about themselves and their business and the students then asking questions. In preparation, speakers are presented with a list of typical questions a week or so prior to their scheduled appearance. As I scanned the list of questions, most appeared to be of the nature that I could easily answer on the spot:

- What do you look for in an employee?
- What's the best and worst thing about your job?
- What did you think you wanted to be when you were in high school? (Answer: A Major League Baseball player until I hit .222 my senior season; on to Plan B!)

Then a question caught my eye that I had to think long and hard about. "What's the best piece of advice you have ever received?"

My answer took me back over two decades. Although I didn't realize it at the time, I was on the management fast track early in my career. One day a senior manager known for his rather gruff exterior called me into his office and informed me that the company wanted to transfer me and my young family to another state to manage a factory. This was a rather large (and scary) leap for someone who had only worked in a sterile engineering department up to that point.

Over the course of the next couple of weeks, I learned that the gruff manager had a soft side as he coached me through my concerns. He patiently walked me through every line of the company's financial statements until I could explain each back to him. He assured me that the company wouldn't put me in a situation where I wouldn't be successful. In short, he prepared me for the challenge both mentally and emotionally.

I finally accepted the offer and was preparing to leave on my adventure when he called me into his office one last time. "I have one other thing I want you to do before leaving," he informed me. "I've seen people lose themselves as they rise through an organization. I want you to spend some time by yourself and write down your values, what you stand for. Then put that list somewhere where you can always find it!"

I followed his advice and created the following list:

■ Never compromise moral or ethical standards for the sake of profit...be honest!
■ Be a husband and a father first. (I later added "and a grandfather.")
■ Don't worry about compensation; do a good job and it will take care of itself.
■ Be fair to yourself; take time off and do things you enjoy.
■ Face difficult situations first and head-on.
■ Tell people when they do a good job.
■ Help make team members promotable.
■ Keep in touch with the people who do the real work.
■ Keep in touch with customers.
■ Give employees advice on decisions when appropriate; once made, support their decision.

My list has stood up well over the course of time with only minor tweaks. As my mentor predicted, I referred to my list multiple times over the course of my career, including when I decided I couldn't climb any higher on the management ladder within that original organization and remain a happy person.

So there it is, the best advice I've received. If you don't already have such a list, I suggest you create one. Hopefully someday you'll agree it was time well spent and will pass that advice on to the next generation of leaders.

Application Challenges

■ Find some quiet time during your next vacation to document your personal principles; keep the list where it is easily accessible.

Reference

1. Brimeyer, Richard D. 2008. *5S Leader's Field Guide: Practical Advice for Establishing a Healthy 5S Culture Within Your Organization*. Story City, IA: PDG Consultants, Inc.

Chapter 10

October—Building a Perpetual Improvement Machine: Daily Improvements, Mistake Proofing, and Problem Solving

There are three mechanisms for implementing Lean improvements depicted below in what I call the "improvement pyramid," as shown in Figure 10.1.

At the peak of the pyramid are rapid improvement events which most readers no doubt associate with Lean. A team of experts are assembled for multiple days and charged with analyzing a specific process, identifying waste, and building a better way.

Properly facilitated, rapid improvement events can be significantly impactful both in terms of the process improvements implemented as well as the growth of team members. A byproduct of events is the confidence and knowledge gained that members often take back to their daily jobs. Rapid improvement events are staff-intensive and this tends to limit their frequency.

Numerous targeted Lean tools may be used inside of a rapid improvement event. These include swim lane mapping, creating flow cells, total productive maintenance

Figure 10.1   The improvement pyramid.

(TPM), quick changeover, process planning (2P), product and process planning (3P), visual inventory control (kanban)...the list goes on and on.

Because only certain tools will be applicable to each expedition, we won't go into detail here on each tool in order to avoid overproduction waste. Explorers headed into the Amazonian rain forest don't need to learn about altitude sickness; those climbing Mount Everest could care less about poisonous snakes. This is the territory for the guide. As a Lean leader, it's not necessary to be an expert on each tool or event planning and facilitation. (By the way, a worthy guide will help identify and transfer these skills to internal experts so that the organization does not remain "hostage" to the guide's knowledge.)

In the middle of our pyramid are good, old-fashioned projects. Oftentimes, various barriers exist which prevent improvements from being implemented within a weeklong rapid improvement event. Perhaps equipment must be specified and procured, software created or modified, or stakeholders require time to seamlessly transition to the change. Projects tend to be capital intensive or dependent on support resources (e.g., the IT department) and so available funding or staffing tends to limit their use.

Books focused on project management skills are abundant. Like rapid improvement event facilitation skills, the success of one's Lean expedition is not contingent on the leader being an expert project manager. It is only important that project management skills exist within the organization or a trusted external resource.

A couple of quick warnings regarding projects, particularly those regarding technology: It is the leader's responsibility to ensure that the "breakthrough" software or technology upgrade doesn't simply automate waste. Also, thoroughly understand the flexibility of the proposed new technology. Too often, organizations find they are handcuffed to virtual monuments with the software or automation chosen severely limiting future improvements.

The base of the improvement pyramid is managing for daily improvement (MDI). These are the "organic" improvements resulting from an entire workforce of engaged employees making frequent small improvements within their respective spheres of influence.

Many will be tiny but, as a former mentor used to advise, "Peanuts are filling." Some may save only a couple of seconds, but perhaps to a process repeated thousands of times per year. A few will be huge, perhaps rivaling the magnitude of benefit realized from a rapid improvement event.

Unlike rapid improvement events and projects, daily improvements are essentially limitless. They depend only on the level of employee engagement and culture…two factors heavily influenced by leaders. That's also why, unlike rapid improvement events and projects, responsibility for MDI cannot be outsourced. It resides squarely on our shoulders.

It only makes sense that we devote a month to the general topic of improvements initiated by individuals. We'll start with an overview of MDI. Then we'll delve into the specific leadership behaviors for promoting MDI.

Next, we'll take a look at mistake proofing which can be used in an individual or a team setting to prevent defects. Think of mistake proofing as a specific type of a daily improvement focused solely on quality.

We'll finish up with some thoughts on developing employees into problem solvers. Perhaps no other skill is more valuable to a successful Lean expedition since it is so encompassing. Skillful problem solving results in better daily improvements and more effective mistake proofs that address the root causes (as opposed to symptoms) of real problems.

The insightful reader will notice that we've come full circle. Once again, we are discussing Lean culture as much or more than the tools themselves. Fortunately, all of the leader attitudes and behaviors discussed during our first seven months compliment MDI, mistake proofing and solving problems.

More importantly, employing these tools allow employees to operate at the highest levels of Maslow's pyramid (esteem and self-actualization), resulting in higher engagement and more daily improvements. That sounds like a virtuous cycle!

Week 40 – Getting a Little Better Each Day

It is the ultimate cliché. Athletes and CEOs state it all the time, "We just need to get a little better each day."

Lean gurus refer to it as MDI, but most "experts" offer little practical advice as to how one goes about actually creating a workplace where every employee is continually making incremental improvements…a truly Lean culture.

Thus, I was intrigued to listen to Paul A. Akers at the Iowa Lean Consortium's 2016 Fall Conference discuss how he created such an environment. Akers is the founder and president of FastCap LLC (www.fastcap.com), a very successful product development company located in Washington state. Akers is also a world-renowned Lean enthusiast, practicing its principles both in the management of his company and in his personal life. His book *2 Second Lean* is in its 3rd edition.[1]

In order to fully appreciate Akers' lessons, I had a personal hurdle to overcome. Akers is a Lean "celebrity" and I have a natural aversion to celebrities. I would rather have lunch with my own physician, Dr. Matt, than Dr. Oz or Dr. Phil.

I cynically listened as Akers boiled down FastCap's success into three pillars. And I became a believer!

The first is to teach people to see waste. In addition to daily, one-minute reminders on the eight forms of waste, Akers continually encourages folks to identify, "What bugs you?" He reasons that behind every irritant is waste.

The second pillar is to schedule time each day for employees to make improvements. FastCap dedicates the first hour of each workday to making improvements and a company-wide meeting. One hour...every day! That's really managing for daily improvement, not simply wishing for it.

The final pillar is sharing the success stories. FastCap encourages employees to make short before and after videos on their cellphone documenting their improvements. These are shared during the daily meeting. It's an opportunity to recognize the improvers and provide ideas to others.

"That's it?" I wondered. It seems too simple. I concluded that this is another example of where simple doesn't equate to easy.

It's not earth-shattering that if people are expected to make improvements, time has to be set aside for them to do it. It's quite another thing to actually schedule time away from normal activities, to provide training so employees know what to do, and to have accountability processes in place to ensure people are effectively making use of that time.

I decided to put the new information to the test. Beginning with 2017, I tried to implement an improvement each day. For the year I documented 91 improvements. Here's what I've learned so far:

■ "What bugs you?" is a powerful question. Well over 50 percent of my improvements were identified by simply being tuned into personal peeves.

Allow me a quick example: I enjoy swimming laps at the public pool over lunch when working from home and so I purchase a season pass which is a small (3" × 1.5") plastic card with a barcode. Undoubtedly, when it was my turn to be scanned at the admissions booth, I would be digging through the pockets of my pants and swim bag trying to find my pass (motion waste). That bugged me...not to mention the people in line behind me and pool check-in staff (waiting waste).

I had an unused retractable name badge holder so I attached my pass to it and attached the badge holder to my swim bag. Now every time I check in I celebrate my cleverness with a smug smile. I think I've even heard some "oohs" and "ahhs" coming from admiring folks in line.

- Improvements come in all sizes. Many are quite small (e.g., unsubscribing from a nuisance email, converting a regular bill payment to automatic withdrawal, creating a simple Excel template for tracking personal mileage). A few have been big and/or expensive (e.g., cataract surgery). All make my job and/or life better.
- Large improvements can be broken down into smaller projects to fit the scheduled improvement time. 5S the garage can become 5S the workbench, 5S the storage rack, 5S the east wall, etc.
- It's important to keep a list of potential improvements at the ready. Great ideas evaporate when left to memory.
- Not every improvement gets added to the list. Some are easy to overlook, especially when improving becomes a way of life…that's okay!

Getting a little better each day is possible, but it requires significant behavior change beginning with management. Without that commitment, all we're really signing up for is more random variation of good days and bad days. Nothing changes…until something changes.

Application Challenges

- Start documenting your own daily improvements (at-home improvements count). List your own lessons learned.
- Read Paul Aker's *2 Second Lean*.[1] It's a fun read and takes Lean down to its simplest form.

Week 41 – A Recipe for Continuous Improvement

For years I've been very intrigued by the concept of creating an organization where a majority of the employees are motivated and confident in making frequent small improvements within their respective areas of expertise. MDI is generally considered to be the secret sauce for a true Lean culture.

Like most things associated with cooking up a great culture, the majority of the key ingredients for establishing successful MDI must be supplied by management.

The most important management behavior is to be intentional about improvement. This means ensuring regular, specific blocks of time are scheduled for all employees—including all levels of management—to work on improvements. This sends a clear message that improvement is part of the job as opposed to something we do in our free time. Besides, who has free time?

Being deliberate about spending time with employees (i.e., rounding) during or immediately after their scheduled improvement time provides an opportunity to become familiar with new improvements, recognize successes, and address barriers.

It also sends a clear expectation that improvement time is to be used wisely since employees know they will have to make an account for themselves.

Emphasize small improvements that are within each employee's sphere of influence. Sure, occasionally a big project requiring multidisciplinary support and perhaps special funding will surface, but that isn't where we want the primary focus. The goal is daily sustainable improvements. Examples of some of my recent, simple improvements include:

- Removing infrequently used and obsolete keys from my keychain.
- Clearly distinguishing metric tools from their English counterparts in my toolbox.
- Relocating a frequently used utensil to a more convenient location in the kitchen.
- Tweaking a spreadsheet to make it more user-friendly.
- Adding "w/i" (which I frequently use as shorthand for within) to the list of auto-corrections in Microsoft Word so it doesn't automatically change it to "w/I."

Finally, another leadership behavior to promote continuous improvement is to religiously share success stories. This accomplishes two things. First, it recognizes those individuals that are doing the right thing. Second, it provides improvement ideas for others. My keychain improvement above came from another leader sharing this idea.

Employees also must bring some vital ingredients to the daily improvement mix. They should be able to identify waste in their work…those steps in the process which take time and consume resources, but don't positively impact the customer's experience with the product or service. Often, waste can be found by simply being attuned to what bugs you. ("Why do I grab the wrong wrench 90 percent of the time, when there are only two choices? I'm going to mark the metric wrench so it's obvious.")

Once waste is identified, employees need to be inquisitive and not simply accept that's the way it is. They should be willing to ask, "Why?" or "What if…?" This requires that they possess an appropriate balance of an inner drive to challenge the status quo with an ability to recognize their sphere of influence. It also means they should possess a basic problem-solving process.

How does one go about hiring those qualities? By making them part of the selection criteria during the hiring process. Example interview questions might include:

- Tell me about a problem that you recently solved or a process you improved? How did you become aware of the opportunity?
- How do you go about trying to solve a problem?
- What is a small problem or issue that you are currently working on?
- How do you react when a small problem within your control frustrates you?

Establishing a healthy continuous improvement culture isn't rocket science. It's actually simple common sense. The true test is having the confidence, trust and discipline to set aside time regularly for your organization to improve. Based on the rarity of organizations that have mastered continuous improvement, it's safe to say that's not easy.

Application Challenges

■ Devise a small pilot to promote MDI within your area of responsibility using the lessons learned from your own experience. Designate a pilot population. Experiment with scheduling different time periods for improvement (e.g., ten minutes/day, one hour/week). Provide a mechanism for sharing and recognizing successes.

■ If you are not already, include questions during employee rounding to promote employees to think about improvements. For example, "What's keeping you from serving your customers?" or "What could work better?" or simply "What bugs you?" Be careful not to walk away with the problem but rather guide the employee through the process.

■ Review your questions used during interviewing. Are you probing for inquisitiveness?

Week 42 – Mistake Proofing

Mistake proofing recognizes that humans aren't perfect; we all make mistakes. But through the creative design of products, services and processes, those mistakes don't have to turn into product/service defects at the customer. Let's delve deeper into how to implement mistake proofing within your organization.

Before starting, I always use the term "mistake proof" rather than "idiot proof." Over the course of my career, I hired maybe 283 employees. By last count, that total included 0 idiots and 283 humans, all of whom occasionally made mistakes and so could benefit from mistake proofing. Only an idiot would employ a workforce of idiots.

Mistake proofing distinguishes between the cause (error) and the effect (defect). While human errors or mistakes are inevitable, they don't have to result in product/service defects.

First of all, it makes sense to understand the defects which are already escaping to your customers, both external and internal customers. Hopefully, a system is in place to capture customer complaint data. Use that data to identify a high frequency defect.

At this point, we typically call the troops together and announce, "Be careful so you don't forget to…" But, this approach is only effective when the root cause of the error is lack of knowledge, not human fallibility. Therefore, the defect occurs again and again.

For example, the fact that I know I'm supposed to turn off the coffee maker each morning doesn't mean that I will do it 100 percent of the time. A warning message on the machine would be of little use. Instead, the coffee maker is designed to automatically turn off if a certain time or temperature is exceeded, a much more effective mistake proof.

With mistake proofing we use the experts who actually produce the product or service to identify the human error that causes the defect. More often than not, they will know. Once the human error has been identified, the fun and creative work begins. In order of preference, we want to identify an entirely effective means for

- Preventing the specific human error from happening in the first place (Level 1 mistake proof).
- Immediately detecting the human error if it does occur (Level 2).
- Effectively identifying the defect if it occurs (Level 3).

Let's assume we have a call center and workers occasionally forget to complete a required date field on an electronic form. Or perhaps they occasionally mistype and enter an invalid date.

A Level 1 mistake proof might involve improving the form so that workers click on the actual date on a calendar within the field rather than typing the date info. A Level 2 mistake proof might turn the field red immediately and not allow the worker to exit it until a valid date has been entered. A Level 3 mistake proof might inform the worker that the date field contains invalid data when they go to submit the completed form.

Frequently, effective mistake proofs can be implemented at minimal cost. Like identifying the actual error that caused the defect, using the creativity of the folks who actually produce the product or deliver the service to brainstorm and select the mistake proof is highly recommended.

Years ago, a supervisor friend was frustrated by recurring reports of units failing prematurely because an extra thrust waster was included. The washers were about the size and thickness of a large soup can lid except perfectly flat and smooth. My friend took an example of a failed unit to a team meeting, split the group into two teams and challenged them to independently identify the human error which resulted in two washers being assembled and a means to prevent the error.

Both teams agreed that the error was caused by assemblers mistakenly grabbing two washers instead of one. This was exacerbated by the fact that the washers were thin, flat, and tended to stick together due to the oil coating used to prevent rust.

One of the teams came up with a slick idea for a washer dispenser similar to the coin dispensers that car hops used years ago. The washers were loaded into a tube constructed of PVC with a slot at the bottom wide enough to accommodate only a single washer. A few hours and ten bucks later, the idea was being piloted. The team later switched from PVC to steel for the dispenser as they learned that continual use caused the critical slot width to grow when the dispenser was plastic.

Communicating customer feedback and involving workers in eliminating defects provides multiple benefits. Providing defect information reinforces the relevancy of work by sharing the voice of the customer. Involving employees in the mistake proofing process demonstrates that their ideas are valued. Most importantly, it greatly increases the odds of an effective solution by involving those closest to the problem, increasing the size of the idea pool, and ensuring ownership in the solution. That's a winning combination.

Application Challenges

■ Practice mistake proofing on a personal defect. Identify the error (cause) which results in the defect (effect). Try to identify Level 1 (prevent the error), Level 2 (immediately detect the error), and Level 3 (detect the defect) mistake proofs and select one to implement.
■ Regularly display defects. Encourage employee input to identify the human error causing the defect and mistake proofing ideas.

Week 43 – The Importance of Not Knowing

About ten years ago I attended a short training session over breakfast. I don't recall the topic or the speaker being especially effective, but one visual image presented stuck with me.

The presenter used a black-and-white photo of a rowing crew taken 50–60 years ago as an analogy for the workplace of the past. The crew leader shouts instructions via a megaphone. The course is so predictable that the leader isn't even facing forward. The crew requires a limited skillset…the ability to follow instructions and to apply muscle to an oar to propel the racing shell through a static course. (My apologies to competitive rowing members; I'm sure it's a bit more complicated than that.)

For the current workplace the presenter suggested a photo of a two-person kayak negotiating perilous white water. The situation changes constantly. The roar of the water makes all but perhaps one-word communication impossible. This crew must be able to assess an ever-changing situation, adapt, and work together to apply both navigation and propulsion skills to the craft.

So how do we develop kayakers instead of rowers? Start by hiring autonomous thinkers and grow them into confident decision makers and problem solvers. The latter requires that we provide opportunities to solve problems. That means we need to stop solving every problem ourselves.

One of the most important decisions an organization has to make is to determine who should make the decision. Two bad things happen when leaders make decisions and solve problems that should be performed by the people reporting to them.

First, and most obviously, we're hindering the development of our employees. We're essentially placing a glass ceiling above them, one associated with their reporting structure.

Second, by default we're not working on the things we should be. These ignored duties are less urgent but almost always strategic and thus more important to the long-term health of the organization. By overlooking these responsibilities, we place a ceiling on the organization, in effect ensuring the status quo...or worse.

The transition from super solver to curiosity coach is not easy. During a breakout entitled "Management Engagement, the Other Half of the Transformation" at the 2015 Iowa Lean Consortium Fall Conference, fellow Lean consultant Beau Keyte made the distinction of "Who owns the thinking?" When a supervisor directs, analyzes, corrects, or suggests, they own the thinking.

Conversely, when a supervisor asks the right questions to increase the employee's curiosity, instead of leading the employee to the supervisor's conclusion, the employee owns the thinking.

Here's an example of how that might look:

Employee: The automatic sliding door on my minivan stopped working.
Supervisor: Hmm. That's annoying...those things are pretty handy when you have your arms full of groceries or kids. I wonder why.
Employee: Well, it doesn't matter if I use the key fob, the door handle or the dashboard switch so it's not that. I cleaned out the tracks. There were a few Cheerios down there, but nothing that should have jammed it.
Supervisor: Those are good things to check. Are there some other easy things you might try?
Employee: Well...I suppose I should check the fuse. That's easy.
Supervisor: Yeah, good idea.
Employee (later): The fuse was blown. I replaced it and two days later the door stopped working again and I had another blown fuse.
Supervisor: It sounds like you're getting closer. I wonder why the fuse keeps blowing.
Employee: The only other thing on the circuit is the air conditioner compressor.
Supervisor: Only one other thing? That's lucky! How can we figure out for sure whether it's the door or the compressor?
Employee: Fortunately, fuses are dirt cheap. I can activate each independently and see which one blows the fuse. I just thought of something...both of the times the door stopped working was after I ran the defroster which uses the compressor.
Supervisor: That's a good observation. I'll be curious to hear how your test goes.
Employee: Well, the compressor consistently blew the fuse. I did a little internet research on my minivan and it's pretty common for the compressor

bearings to go out at 80,000 miles. I have 85,000. I got under the hood and yanked on the pulley and could even sense some play.

Supervisor: So your door isn't working because your compressor bearings are bad. Who would have thought? Nice job!

The value is in asking the right questions. In addition to growing people, it's actually liberating to not have to be the answer machine.

Application Challenges

■ Ensure that your organization embraces a formal problem-solving process. 8D (8 Disciplines), A3, DMAIC (Define, Measure, Analyze, Improve, and Control) are all possibilities. Embrace and regularly practice the tool on your own problems so that you can guide others through it.

■ Read *Managing to Learn* for an excellent example on how to develop a team of problem solvers.[2]

References

1. Akers, Paul A. 2012. *2 Second Lean: How to Grow People and Build a Fun Lean Culture at Work & at Home.* Ferndale, WA: FastCap Press.
2. Shook, John. 2008. *Managing to Learn: Using the A3 Management Process to Solve Problems, Gain Agreement, Mentor, and Lead.* Cambridge, MA: Lean Enterprise Institute.

Chapter 11

November—The Importance of Stories: Case Studies of Successes

We humans are wired to love stories. From our earliest days of comprehension, parents use stories to teach lessons, reinforce norms, and entertain. The most gifted teachers and leaders use stories to drive lessons deeper into our retention.

Stories are so effective because they elicit both an intellectual and an emotional response. The emotional response sticks with us longer. Variations on an oft-repeated quote remind us, "They may forget what you said—but they will never forget how you made them feel."[1]

Stories also help provide the sense of purpose and sometimes the escape necessary for overcoming the many hurdles inherent to any worthwhile venture. As mentioned in Chapter 1, one of the most fascinating stories that I've listened to is the audio version of Candice Millard's *The River of Doubt* (check it out for your next extended car trip).[2] Millard paints a vivid picture of the exploring party, the majority of who were veterans of numerous epic expeditions, spending nights around the campfire telling stories of prior adventures. The entertainment no doubt provided an escape from their current perilous situation. One can almost hear the storyteller promising, "I've been in worse pinches than this before; we'll make it out of this jam as well."

Likewise, I hope that sharing stories of some of my prior adventures will be educational and inspiring. Perhaps you'll pick up on a subtle point regarding a Lean tool that I inadvertently overlooked during an earlier chapter. Maybe the actions of the leader in the story will reinforce a key behavior for you (e.g., the city manager actually took *two days* out of his busy schedule to participate in a rapid improvement event on paving). Perhaps your expedition has hit an inevitable rough spot and you simply need to be inspired.

As you advance on your Lean expedition, it's extremely beneficial to turn noteworthy improvements and benchmarks attained into your own stories. These provide fuel for future challenges and play a key role in converting fence-sitters to join the effort.

Document your own expedition with stories and photos. It's amazing how quickly one forgets the prior state.

A quick word of warning! As we learned in Chapter 3, Edgar Schein counsels us that stories, legends, and myths about people and events are a secondary embedding mechanism. If our current actions are consistent with the lessons we are teaching or the norms we are reinforcing, our stories will further our intent. If not, our stories will cause cynicism or lead to longing for past days and leaders whose actions were consistent with the moral of the story.

Note that all four of our case studies involve non-manufacturing organizations; two from healthcare, one from municipal government, and one from education. Lean principles are pervasive across all sectors as any organization can benefit from developing engaged waste avengers.

Week 44 – Benefiting All Stakeholders

I've seen a lot of programs, buzzwords, and gimmicks come and go during the course of my 35 years in business. I've also personally witnessed Lean methodologies succeed for almost three decades, and it's been around a lot longer than that.

There's a fundamental reason for that longevity. Lean is unique in that, performed properly, it benefits customers, owners, *and* employees. Other short-lived programs benefited one, maybe two, stakeholders but at the expense of the others. As such, they simply weren't sustainable.

There's no better example of the impact of Lean than a project I completed with Mary Greeley Medical Center (MGMC). This project had amazing results that will provide long-lasting benefits for patients, visitors, the hospital, and medical center staff.

The ability to efficiently and effectively clean and resupply a patient room following a patient discharge is critical to any hospital. Quality is paramount, both in terms of thoroughly disinfecting against invisible germs as well as the very visible aesthetics that impact a patient's first impression at admission.

Speed and productivity follow close behind. Patient room availability is often a key factor in determining patient throughput in feeder processes such as the emergency department, especially during periods of high census. Medicare and insurance reimbursements are based on industry best practices and not actual costs incurred by a specific facility.

Thus, it was only natural that MGMC chose discharge room cleaning for one of their initial rapid improvement events. Team members included three environmental services (ES) workers, two ES managers, two nursing managers from patient floors, and MGMC's Lean coordinator.

We started by analyzing in detail a video of the current process as performed by one of the ES workers, a known top performer. It became immediately obvious that the discharge cleaning process made what we would call a deep clean at home look like child's play.

The opportunities for process variation were mind-numbing:

■ Dozens of discharge room cleans occurred daily across several different patient units.
■ Almost 50 different ES workers performed the task.
■ 188 distinct steps were required to ensure a thorough job.

It was interesting to listen to the comments of the ES team members as they observed the video. Comments such as "Oh, that's a good idea!" or "That's not how I do it," or "Here's a little trick I use to do that," were common.

Two needs became immediately obvious. First, a common definition of a standard clean room was required across patient units. Most patient units had their own self-imposed definitions. Differences were typically based on legacy rather than unique patient needs, although the latter did exist. Figures 11.1 and 11.2 demonstrate the standard for a clean room.

Second, standard work was needed to capture and share best practices of all ES workers. In order to be practical, however, we had to first break down the myriad of individual process steps into a manageable number of subsystems.

Ten "macro" steps such as stripping the room and cleaning the bedside tray were identified and sequenced. See Figure 11.3 for the standard of macro steps. Macro steps facilitate both end-of-shift handoffs ("I got through Step 5.") as well as splitting work when an emergency situation necessitates a team clean ("I've got Step 1; you take Step 2.").

Then each macro step was broken down into the detailed steps in the required sequence to complete the task in the known best method. The liberal use of photographs clearly defined each step and minimized the use of words for each standard. See Figure 11.4 for an example of a detailed standard for cleaning the bed.

Following several rounds of clarifications and process improvements, each standard was finally approved and rolled out to all ES workers following a training session. A laminated copy of the set of standards was provided with each room cleaning cart.

The results have been spectacular:

■ Internal quality checks to determine if various areas of the patient rooms have been thoroughly disinfected jumped significantly to over 99 percent.

Discharge room cleaning
end state-standard room placement

Mary Greeley
MEDICAL CENTER

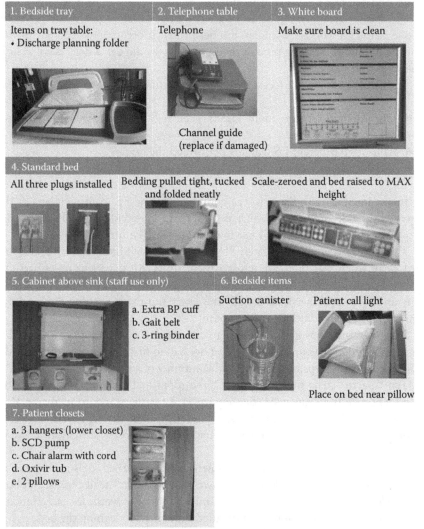

1. Bedside tray	2. Telephone table	3. White board
Items on tray table: • Discharge planning folder	Telephone Channel guide (replace if damaged)	Make sure board is clean

4. Standard bed		
All three plugs installed	Bedding pulled tight, tucked and folded neatly	Scale-zeroed and bed raised to MAX height

5. Cabinet above sink (staff use only)	6. Bedside items	
a. Extra BP cuff b. Gait belt c. 3-ring binder	Suction canister	Patient call light Place on bed near pillow

7. Patient closets
a. 3 hangers (lower closet) b. SCD pump c. Chair alarm with cord d. Oxivir tub e. 2 pillows

Figure 11.1   Standard for a clean patient room.

Discharge room cleaning
standard room items

Mary Greeley

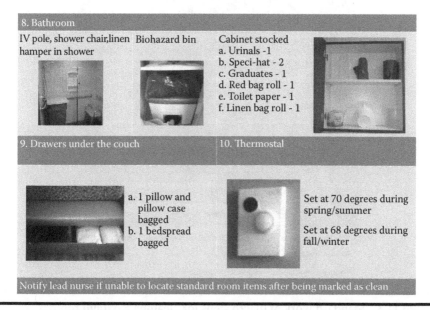

8. Bathroom

IV pole, shower chair,linen Biohazard bin
hamper in shower

Cabinet stocked
a. Urinals -1
b. Speci-hat - 2
c. Graduates - 1
d. Red bag roll - 1
e. Toilet paper - 1
f. Linen bag roll - 1

9. Drawers under the couch | **10. Thermostal**

a. 1 pillow and pillow case bagged
b. 1 bedspread bagged

Set at 70 degrees during spring/summer

Set at 68 degrees during fall/winter

Notify lead nurse if unable to locate standard room items after being marked as clean

Figure 11.2 Standard for a clean patient room (continued).

- Patient exit survey scores responding positively to a question regarding room cleanliness improved significantly and now place MGMC in the top 25 percent of hospitals in this category.
- The average time to complete a discharge clean dropped and the process is no longer recognized as a bottleneck for making rooms available to new patients; variation in time also decreased.
- Turnover among ES Staff over the past year dropped to less than half of what it was in the prior three years.

The last metric excites me the most. Standard work provides ES workers with confidence that they—and their coworkers—are completing the task consistently by the known best method. They are much less apt to become the scapegoat as hospital staff wait for a room to be available for a new patient.

ES workers continued to make improvements to the standards as new ideas emerged (more on that soon). They even requested standard work be completed for other repetitive tasks: the daily freshening up of rooms required during a patient

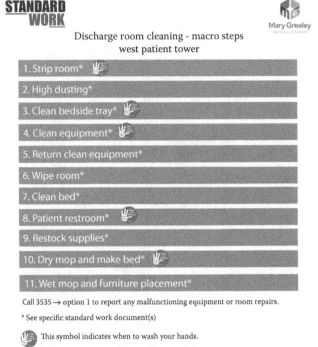

Figure 11.3 Standard work of macro steps for cleaning a patient room.

stay, cleaning of operating rooms between surgeries and cleaning of whirlpool baths on the birthing floor.

Safer and satisfied patients, lower medical costs, and happier employees...now that's sustainable!

Application Challenges

■ Establish a *simple* improvement database. It's easy to forget what you've accomplished on your expedition.

■ Develop some compelling stories of successful improvements within your organization. Without embellishing, share the benefits for various stakeholders (customers, employees, and owners/funders). Recognize those who worked hard to make the improvement possible. Finally, tell the stories often.

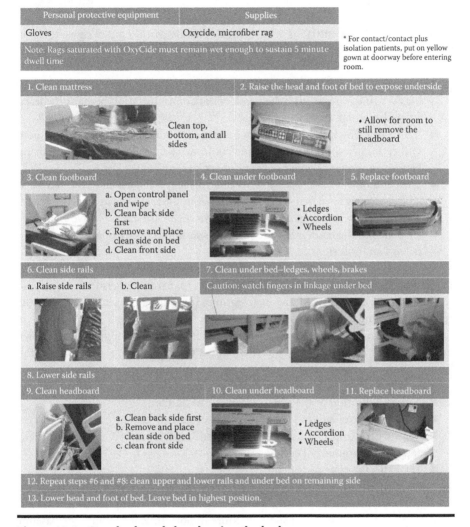

Figure 11.4   Standard work for cleaning the bed.

Week 45 – The Rest of the Story

We're all familiar with the wooden box located in the lunchroom entitled "Employee Suggestions." You know, the one gathering dust. The one where great ideas go to die.

Let's start by identifying the typical pitfalls with employee suggestion systems:

- The process for submitting ideas is impersonal and rife with misunderstanding. Writing is a one-way, shallow form of communication perhaps the least-favored method for most employees.
- A terrible thing happens as the suggestion slip slides through the slot; responsibility for the improvement transfers from the employee to management. Now it's a matter of whether "they" want to do it.
- The decision-making process for evaluating suggestions is slow and flawed as it often occurs by managers far-removed from the real issue during an agenda-filled monthly meeting, unwilling to leave the board room to investigate it.
- Feedback to the employee is frequently as slow and impersonal as the submittal and analysis steps.

So how do we create an improvement system that is more personal, timely and results in better decisions? Many organizations are finding the secret lies with successfully implementing standard work.

Standard work is defined as the documented (preferably through photos) known best process for completing a critical, repetitive task. It typically contains the following pieces of information required to successfully complete a process:

- A clear definition of the expected output or outcome
- The sequence of steps in the appropriate order
- The "stuff" (tools, supplies, information, and inventory) needed and the appropriate amount of each
- The expected time to complete

Once implemented in an area, standard work is *the* training document for the process, providing training consistency. More importantly, it becomes the baseline against which future suggested improvements are measured.

In a healthy environment, employees are constantly challenged to use their creativity and knowledge to improve standard work. Ideas are discussed with one's supervisor at the place where the work actually occurs. A real-time decision is made together on whether the idea warrants testing and, if so, how an objective, data-based evaluation can be completed. If not, the employee clearly understands that their idea was heard and the criteria for the decision. Regardless of whether their idea is pursued, they are recognized for using their noodle.

If the suggestion indeed results in a better process, standard work is revised to reflect the change and all impacted employees are trained on the revision, thus resulting in an improved process for everyone...not just the person who had the idea.

The ES team at MGMC utilized standard work to document the current best method for cleaning patient rooms following a discharge. Prior to standard work, cleaning process variation was significant due to the number of different workers, different patient units, and the fact that almost 200 steps were required to thoroughly clean a room.

Documented results from both in-house testing and patient surveys showed a notable improvement in the quality of room cleans. The team also experienced productivity improvements as the average time to clean a room dropped and became more consistent among workers.

But here's the really cool part: standard work provided the vehicle for continuously improving the cleaning process. In less than two years, roughly 50 improvement suggestions were implemented to the cleaning process! That's an average of two improvements per month by a single team on a single work activity—cleaning patient rooms.

In fact, the team decided to stop laminating the standard work booklets provided with each cleaning cart. Because the process was improving so rapidly, managers identified the lamination step as extra-processing waste. They also reasoned that lamination sent an unwanted message to some employees, suggesting the standard was intended to be permanent.

Fifty improvements in less than two years impacting a single process! Those are numbers suggestion boxes can't match. Imagine that power unleashed across your entire organization.

Application Challenge

■ Audit some of your standard work documents. What is the demonstrated frequency for improvement revisions? Is the frequency consistent with a continuous improvement culture?

Week 46 – Pursuing Excellence While Patching

In the fall of 2009, a team came together for two days to identify ways to improve concrete patching within the City of Fort Dodge. The team consisted of maintenance workers and managers from public works and other departments, including the city manager.

While large street resurfacing projects were contracted out, smaller patching jobs were historically split between city workers and local contractors. The city hoped that, by improving their productivity, a larger percentage of patching jobs could be completed by city employees, thus reducing external spending.

The team started by taking a hard look at the processes they currently used. This included data collected from the recently completed patching season.

They also viewed a video tape from a recent patching job. The video showed several instances of multiple workers leaning on shovels and watching as a couple of coworkers performed a task. Everyone in the room was sensitive to the stereotype; watching it play out on a video wasn't particularly pleasant.

But a wonderful thing happened as the team critically analyzed their current methods. They began to realize that each patching job was made up of a number of repetitive steps: prepping the job, breaking up the bad section of street, removing the bad material, setting forms, etc. These various steps had widely varying labor demands. For example, breaking up concrete could be safely accomplished by a single worker, while pouring concrete required all hands on deck.

The practice for assigning workers had always been to send the entire crew needed to satisfy the peak demand step (pouring concrete) out for the entire project. Thus, the number of busy (and idle) workers cycled as the job moved from one step to the next. Workers leaning on shovels wasn't a statement of work ethic…it was the result of a less-than-ideal scheduling process.

The excitement grew as the team started to define how things could look differently during 2010. Supervisors agreed they could schedule workers by process step rather than by job. The team defined each distinct process step and the number of workers required to safely and effectively complete it.

In order to take full advantage of this strategy, the city would have multiple projects occurring simultaneously so that workers could move to another project during a non-peak step. The team realized this was possible so long as they minimized the time when a street was impassable for drivers. Many of the prep and finishing steps could occur several days before or after the required shutdown of the street with no impact to traffic flow.

The old way of scheduling was pretty straightforward…work one project at a time and send out the whole crew. The new method involved much more communication and coordination between multiple jobs. To help keep everyone on the same page, an unused white board was converted into a large visual calendar, providing real time updates of job status and assignments.

The results were amazing. During 2010, city workers patched almost three times as much area as they had in 2009. The city eliminated all contracting of patching jobs, saving tens of thousands of dollars.

But the improvement didn't stop there. Following the 2010 season, employees got back together to discuss lessons learned. It was noted that the streets department could do a better job of working with the engineering department to prioritize and schedule jobs for the upcoming season. This allowed for a more realistic schedule and for jobs to be better timed for minimal disruption to traffic.

The streets department also recognized that they had been overly ambitious in taking on a large project in a low-lying area. The project drug on for weeks when constant drainage into the job site during the wet summer made conditions unworkable. Future projects in similar areas would be broken up into several smaller jobs.

Crews set another record in 2011, topping 2010 by another 40 percent. Again, lessons learned following the season identified further improvements. 2012 saw yet another record, topping the prior year by 2 percent or 4.2 times the amount accomplished in 2009 with the same number of employees.

Improvements such as this are possible when teams commit to excellence. And when management recognizes that mediocre performance almost always results from bad processes, not bad people.

Application Challenge

■ The streets department celebrated a record-breaking construction season with a chicken dinner. Are you appropriately stopping to celebrate noteworthy efforts?

Week 47 – Stimulus Success Story

During the 2012 campaign season, candidates vigorously debated the merits of two huge government programs resulting from the Great Recession:

■ The $700 billion Emergency Economic Stabilization Act of 2008, popularly known as the Bank Bailout, which resulted in the Troubled Asset Relief Program
■ The $800 billion American Recovery and Reinvestment Act of 2009 (ARRA), also known as the Stimulus Bill

While I don't want to revisit the politics of these programs (my nightmares from the campaign just recently stopped), I'd like to share how a popular organization made great use of stimulus funds.

4-H Youth Development is the iconic branch of Iowa State University Extension and Outreach. 4-H's primary focus over the years had been on the *content* of the materials used for their various learning projects. As a result, they realized that the *processes* for producing and delivering those materials were lacking.

During the latter half of 2009, 4-H applied for and received $25,000 ARRA funding to explore and implement Lean methods. During 2010 they utilized the funding to contract with me to develop managers on leading a Lean culture and to facilitate three rapid improvement events. These activities resulted in significant savings and fundamentally changed how 4-H works.

One of the rapid improvement events addressed an improved process for delivering project materials, the educational resources which 4-H provides to its members to support their learning activities.

4-H's decades-old paradigm was to purchase booklets from National 4-H. Roughly 175 different titles, from beginning dairy to advanced robotics, existed to cover the wide range of interests and skills levels required to meet the needs of 4-H members.

A team of nine experts from across the state, representing all levels of the organizational chart, came together to find a better way. Working as equals for three days, they designed a new process which resulted in a significant win-win for members, their families, and the 4-H organization.

The team started by identifying what their customers desired from project materials. This activity uncovered the facts that today's youth prefer online learning to books, and that their families expect free, instant access to information that doesn't require a trip into town during regular office hours.

Next, the current process was mapped in detail. Tens of thousands of booklets were printed nationally (based on a forecast) and stored in a warehouse in the Washington, DC area. State organizations, such as ISU Extension and Outreach 4-H, placed an annual order for the publications they anticipated needing. These were stored on campus and delivered to county 4-H offices when ordered. Members' families finally made the trip to the local office to pick up booklets.

Waste in the current process was noted:

■ ISU Extension and Outreach 4-H placed an annual order for roughly 20,000 booklets, costing almost $100,000, with the majority of this expense recouped as project materials were resold to members.
■ Like any forecast, however, there were invariably stock-outs, resulting in members anxiously waiting for materials to start their project.
■ Like any forecast, there was also overstock. The campus distribution warehouse held over 90,000 booklets worth almost $300,000 that had accumulated over the years.
■ Enormous resources were required at every level of 4-H to manage the production, distribution, and inventory of booklets.

The team designed a new process built around internet access to project materials. Follow-up meetings and projects were required to implement the necessary changes to the 4-H website and to ensure that all project materials were research-based, as ensured by the ISU Extension and Outreach brand.

The team's dream became reality within several months and 4-H members and their families began receiving 24/7, instant access to project materials at a fraction of the cost of booklets.

The following year, the team was recognized and asked to tell their story at the 4-H North Central Regional Conference. Today, their solution is becoming the benchmark nationally.

This single project resulted in an annual savings two to three times the one-time $25,000 ARRA funding. The two other rapid improvement events delivered similar, but smaller benefits. 4-H took advantage of the situation to develop an internal resource to lead future improvement activities.

Better customer service and a great return on investment—that's something any businessperson would be proud of (and any politician would gladly claim personal responsibility for).

Application Challenges

■ Have you extended Lean into your back-office (i.e. support) processes?

References

1. *Quote Investigator.* 2014. They May Forget What You Said, But They Will Never Forget How You Made Them Feel. https://quoteinvestigator.com/2014/04/06/they -feel/#return-note-8611-1 (accessed Dec. 20, 2017).
2. Millard, Candice. 2005. *The River of Doubt: Theodore Roosevelt's Darkest Journey.* New York: Doubleday Broadway Publishing Group.

Chapter 12

December—A Glimpse at the Goal: Case Studies from a Lean Culture

In the Preface I attributed the majority of my consulting success to the 25 years I spent with my first employer, the predecessor companies of what is today called Danfoss Power Systems. It was extremely fortuitous to have spent multiple early years in a traditional manufacturing environment and to witness and participate firsthand in the transformation to a Lean culture, especially as a young supervisor and manager.

Thus, all of the following case studies are from that organization. They all reflect aspects of a mature Lean organization. Once again, my goal is to educate and inspire with an eye on leadership's role in the successes.

We start with a story that conveys an important aspect of a true participatory and team environment, the ability for *every* member to fearlessly suggest improvements. The fact that the story takes place in the woods during a two-day team building exercise probably says as much about the culture as the story itself. The clarity with which I remember the lesson learned during the exercise is a testament to the effectiveness of experiential learning.

Next, I share a 5S success despite several unique challenges. I focus on the behaviors of the five managers whose departments shared the impacted workspace. It's often said that what gets measured gets done. The five managers ensured that 5S was "measured" via daily audits until they were sure habits were changed and a new status quo was working for them rather than against them. At that point responsibilities for the daily audits were delegated to various employees within the department, resulting in true horizontal accountability. The managers shifted to auditing the audits.

It's one thing to make significant improvements to value streams for existing products and services. But it's even better to develop value streams with minimal waste from the get-go for new products and services. Designing products and processes for quality requires a prevention mindset and faith that (poor) quality truly is the fundamental driver of cost. Incorporating Lean principles into the product development phases is a clear hallmark of a mature Lean organization.

Once one's own house is beginning to run relatively smoothly, a logical extension is to begin expanding Lean efforts with customers and suppliers. In fact, waste *between* our organization and our suppliers and customers will likely be identified as a frustrating barrier to further improvement by adept employees as we progress on our Lean expedition. I share a case study on extended value stream mapping, a mature Lean tool to be worked with customers and suppliers—to the shared mutual benefit of all partners.

We finish up the year with the story of an exceptional Lean leader. I encourage you to take advantage of some time off during the final week to reflect on the progress of your organization during the past year and on your personal growth.

Best wishes as you continue the expedition!

Week 48 – Harvesting Great Ideas

Although it took place roughly 20 years ago, the lesson is seared into my mind like the brand on a cow's rear flank...

My peer team of managers was attending teamwork training, the outdoor experiential kind. As our challenge was being described to us by the event's facilitators, I felt like a kid on Christmas morning. We were to split into sub-teams with each sub-team handed a compass and a map on which various points were designated. We were to use our orienteering skills to find the points hidden among the camp's 1100 acres of rugged wilderness along the Des Moines River. Each point earned us supplies that we would use to build a raft to float our team. Based on the number of team members floated and maneuvers completed on the raft we would earn "revenue" for our fictitious "company."

This was right up my alley! I love hiking. Maps, compasses, and knot tying were specialties of mine as an Eagle Scout. I couldn't believe I was getting paid to have so much fun.

Our sub-team consisted of three engineering managers and our administrative assistant Deb. I gave the group a quick lesson in orienteering.

We divided up targeted points among the sub-teams and took off. Our initial point was located in an open field relatively close to our "headquarters" cabin. We determined the bearing and distance from the map, used the compass to select a landmark in the correct direction and counted our paces. Voilà! There was the four-inch red square with a white letter attached to the trunk of tree, hidden below the tall grass.

A quick celebration ensued and we selected our next target. "We've got this!" we declared.

We set our attention on our second point, again getting our bearing and distance from the map (roughly a half mile). This time, however, our journey took us into the woods so we had to opt for an intermediate target on the edge of the forest, perhaps 100 yards away. Once there, we reasoned, we would pick another landmark and proceed to our mark in multiple segments.

As we advanced into the woods, however, the growth became thicker and thicker. Our segments grew shorter and shorter due to limited visibility. Once a landmark was established, we could no longer walk directly to it due to thickets. Exactly which tree was our target again? Still, we kept our heads down and struggled forward, burning an hour of valuable time.

We even tried creating our own landmark, tying a bandana on the end of a long stick and swinging it as the compass person lined it up in what we now hoped was the correct direction. Our segments were down to 15 yards.

Relatively quiet up to this point, Deb spoke up, "Guys this is crazy! There has to be a better way! We arbitrarily chose the last point as our starting point because we knew where we were. Can't we find a distinct landmark on this map that's much closer to our target and start from there?"

Silence. Three engineering managers sheepishly stared at our feet as lightbulbs flashed above our heads. We had literally lost the forest in the trees. Our initial success further cemented our paradigm. Finally, someone muttered, "I think that's a really good idea."

We looked at our topographical map and noted a ridge coming to a point not 30 yards from the target. If we could find that rather distinct feature it would be much easier to shoot a new line from there to our target as opposed to trying to follow our current course through the Amazon jungle for another quarter mile.

Fifteen minutes later we were celebrating the capture of our second point. More importantly, we had developed an improved process for locating future points. We radioed the other sub-teams to share our lessons learned.

We might still be wandering through the thicket if we hadn't previously established a culture on our team where Deb felt safe sharing a critical observation and an idea. Just as importantly, an environment that recognized that managers don't have the monopoly on good ideas and that each idea deserves a respectful hearing, evaluation, and response.

You never know where your next great idea is coming from...but if you place limits on people you know where it won't come from.

Application Challenge

■ Where do ideas that get implemented originate within your organization? Can you point to a recent improvement which started from each of your employees?

Week 49 – Sustaining the Gains

A while back I accepted an opportunity to facilitate a 5S event on the Engineering Garage at my former employer of 25 years, Danfoss Power Solutions. While I relish chances to work with old friends at Danfoss and enjoy the immediate feedback that accompanies a 5S event, I was nervous about this one.

First, a quick review of 5S. 5S is a tool for creating and maintaining an organized, clean workplace where problems (e.g., missing supplies, inventory shortages) become immediately and visually obvious. 5S is so named because its five distinct phases all begin with the letter S:

■ *Sort:* Remove all of the "stuff" from the work area that doesn't support the job.
■ *Showcase:* Return the work area to a good-as-new condition.
■ *Set in Order:* Return all of the survivors of the sort phase to the work area, selecting the absolute best location for each.
■ *Standardize:* Create new cleanliness standards and make it visually obvious where everything belongs so that it gets returned to the right spot...every time.
■ *Sustain:* Establish new habits to uphold the first four phases every day.

The first three steps are basically followed each time we clean a garage or closet at home. But those efforts are typically in vain as invariably the area is allowed to slowly slip back to its former disorganized and dirty state.

The last two steps therefore make 5S unique. Establishing clear, visual standards to define the new state and ensuring the discipline of everyone who comes in contact with the area to follow the standards.

It was the last two steps that worried me with the Engineering Garage. I had no doubt that we could make a dramatic improvement during the event. But could we sustain it?

While standardize and sustain are always a challenge, my history with Danfoss told me that the Engineering Garage would be especially trying:

■ Five different teams routinely share the work space, thus providing ample opportunity for finger pointing whenever a mess is left.
■ "Outsiders," including customers and employees from other departments occasionally perform work in the garage; these individuals have little ownership for maintaining improvements.
■ Working on hydraulic systems for off-highway vehicles is inherently messy.

Four years later, I'm happy to report that my fears were unfounded. The Engineering Garage routinely looks as good as or better today than it did at the report-out immediately following our event. The success isn't due to any special secrets which I unveiled during the event. Rather, it's a direct result of the dedicated efforts of the five managers and their employees. Their actions provide some valuable lessons for sustaining any improvement.

First of all, all five managers cleared their busy calendars and were full participants during the entire four-day event. They each volunteered key team members to also be full participants. They thus supported the effort with their most critical resource: time.

The managers routinely augmented my teaching with powerful, personal comments as to how important it was to their team and to the company as a whole to create and maintain a cleaner, more organized garage. They made funds available when purchases were needed for items to store tools and supplies in a more orderly manner. Both their actions and their words spoke volumes regarding the importance they associated with the project.

The true extent of their commitment, however, became obvious after the event. Each of the five managers agreed to sign up for a week to perform a detailed, daily audit of the garage at the end of the workday. Using digital photos, they distributed a daily report reinforcing desired behaviors and noting opportunities for further improvement (Figure 12.1).

By the end of the five weeks new habits were being established, and various employees, hungry to maintain the improved work area, volunteered to take over auditing. Today, with very rare exceptions, the area is in a perpetual "tour ready" state even as the regular work of overhauling hydraulic systems occurs.

The very nature of progress begins with leaders having the vision to elevate normal. Improvements are realized by leaders trusting their employees to find a better way and by making resources available. Finally, gains are sustained through leaders' courage and commitment.

The good:

The garage area was "show ready" at the end of the day. Carts, tools, chairs, etc. were back in thier designated spot. The machine work areas were made neat and tidy after everyone else went home. Nice work!

The bad:

1. A broken broom was not taken out of service. I'll get one today.
2. The air gun near the parts washer needs a hook. I'll get one today.
3. Some shelf parts found a nook to hide in.

The ugly:

Couldn't find any ugly. The place looks great!

Figure 12.1 Feedback from daily 5S audit.

Application Challenges

- Return to your home 5S project. Are your sort, showcase, set in order, and standardize improvements being sustained? Don't expect successful sustained 5S from your team until you can answer "Yes!" for your own project.

Week 50 – Perfect Products and Services in an Imperfect World

Several years ago, the company I was working for was informed by a major customer that our quality needed to improve…by a factor of ten.

Our initial reaction was denial. "We're supplying complex transmissions to them with a defect rate of a quarter of a percent. That's 99.75 percent good. They don't know what they're asking!"

The customer patiently explained that their tractors contained thousands of components. If every component was supplied at a 0.25 percent defective rate, statistics predicted that each tractor would roll off the line with several defects. That was clearly unacceptable to their customers.

It quickly became evident that arguing was futile. We had to get to work. How in the heck were we going to ship products with a defect rate of 0.025 percent or 99.975 percent good?

The solution, like so many in business, involved both changes in how we did things (i.e., the tools we used) as well as how we thought about things (i.e., our culture). And the changes had to start with leadership.

Mistake proofing is a Lean tool which recognizes the difference between errors and defects. Errors cause defects. Put another way, the error is the input; the defect is the resultant output.

Unfortunately, errors are unavoidable when working with humans. Sure, they can be reduced through solid hiring practices, proper training, and a good working environment. But ultimately "to err is human."

But (and here's the key point) errors do not have to result in defects. By using the creativity of team members, simple mistake proofs can frequently be implemented to keep errors from turning into defects. Good mistake proofs are:

- 100-percent effective (catching every incident of a particular error).
- Objective (not subject to interpretation).
- Immediate in their feedback.
- Low cost (typically less than $100).

Let me provide a quick example. Occasionally I send emails inadvertently with a blank "Subject:" field. This is considered unprofessional because it doesn't provide the reader with any context as to the urgency of the correspondence. Therefore, the defect (or output) is an email with a blank "Subject:" field. The input or error is me getting so caught up in writing the message that I forget to fill in the subject.

My first attempt at eliminating this defect was to change the order in which I write emails. I tried to fill in the "Subject:" field first, body second, and address list last (which also avoids those embarrassing situations when a partially-completed email is sent). This reduced the number of emails with missing subjects but, because success relied totally on following my new habit (and occasionally I slipped back into my old ways), it didn't completely solve the problem.

I was pleasantly surprised to find that the updated email software I recently purchased contains an effective mistake proof. Now when I hit "Send" with a blank "Subject:" field, I am immediately informed and encouraged to add one (the fact that I know this happens is a testament to the effectiveness of the mistake proof and not because I read the owner's manual).

As mentioned above, changes in thinking (culture) were also required. For mistake proofing to flourish, human errors have to be identified, even embraced, so that they can be guarded against. We had to make it okay, even desirable, to admit, "I just committed an error; let's figure out how to make that impossible."

We had to change an attitude which accepted a certain level of defects as okay. Some of this was a legacy of our formal education in which we were trained to believe that anything above 90 percent is an "A." Instead of thinking in terms of percent (defects per hundred), we needed to think in terms of defects per million.

Finally, and most importantly, we had to change how we designed products and processes. If an error could be conceived during the design phase, we made changes to eliminate that possibility. Quality became *the* primary design consideration. This ultimately resulted in the lowest-cost design since defects are incredibly and deceptively expensive.

A year after I left the company, I received a call from a former colleague over lunch. He informed me that they were celebrating one year of shipments of a new transmission that our team had designed for our challenging customer without a single defect. That's 12,000 units, with roughly 150 components in each unit and every single one perfect!

Application Challenges

■ Is quality *the* primary criteria in the design of your products and/or services?

Week 51 – Improving with Customers

I've facilitated over 250 formal improvement events over the past 13 years. One of the most challenging improvement activities was also one of the most rewarding… funny how that works out.

While working for Sauer-Danfoss (now Danfoss Power Solutions) we supplied a custom-designed transmission to a well-known tractor manufacturer. Orders from the customer were very sporadic—periods of lax orders, followed by requested emergency partial truck shipments were the norm. The crazy orders resulted in our on-time delivery being below both our and the customer's goal.

How could this be? Due to its popularity with consumers, our transmission was practically a standard component on the tractor, included on over 90 percent of the units sold. The output of the assembly line simply couldn't vary that much day-to-day. Our frustration reached a breaking point when we were informed that no units were required from us for the next several weeks due to an inventory build-up at the customer. Now what to do with two shifts with a half-dozen workers apiece and no demand for six weeks?

We agreed that we had to work an improvement project with the customer...a bit of an awkward situation since they were the customer. We first had to overcome the paradigm that the customer is always right.

Fortunately, aside from their erratic ordering patterns, we had an excellent relationship with the customer. We collaborated closely during the design of the innovative transmission whose features set their tractor apart from its competitors.

We always accepted the fact that they hired us for our transmission design expertise. In this case, we reasoned that they now needed us for our supply chain expertise. We had a good ten-year head start in practicing Lean principles.

Value stream mapping is a Lean tool which takes a high-level look at the chain of processes linked within a facility—from the receiving dock to the shipping dock in the case of a factory—to produce a product or service. It addresses the waste which often occurs *between* departments, perhaps after years of focused sub-optimization *within* the individual processes.

Extended value stream mapping takes an even bigger picture view to remove the waste *between* facilities. If the opportunity for suboptimization is significant between departments within the same facility, the prospect across facilities from multiple companies is enormous!

Our visit to the customer's tractor assembly line confirmed our suspicions. Output was 100 tractors per day, plus or minus five...every day. The root cause for their crazy order patterns was a computer-based ordering system which no one really understood.

The customer defined the minimum and maximum number of transmissions they wanted to have on hand. We designed and painted a floor template so pallets of transmissions were always stored in the same place and counting the number of loads on-hand was a cinch. At the end of each workday one of the customer's material handlers communicated to us the actual number of units on hand. For the first time ever, we received a clean signal of what the customer actually had instead of a computer-calculated value based on an algorithm created by Rube Goldberg.

Based on the customer's actual inventory, our shipping team removed the appropriate number of pallets of finished transmissions from a small "supermarket" and loaded them onto a trailer that the trucking company kept at our plant. When the trailer was a day from being filled we notified the trucking company that a driver would be needed the following day for shipment. The assembly cell then built new units to replace the empty spots in the supermarket.

Simple! In essence, each day we built the number of transmissions required to replace those assembled into tractors at the customer's factory 1000 miles away. The solution was a smashing success:

- The customer's average inventory was significantly reduced, freeing up cash and saving space.
- Partial truck shipments were eliminated, saving the customer thousands of dollars in annual shipping costs.
- We realized level demand, avoiding unnecessary overtime and occasional worker surpluses.
- Our on-time delivery went to 100 percent.

Perhaps the biggest benefit, however, was that the cause of animosity towards the customer was eliminated. Everyone involved with the tractor transmission was now connected to our customer. Walking through the factory one day, I noticed the transmission assembly cell wasn't working. When I asked one of the workers who typically worked the cell, he explained that a squirrel had gotten into a transformer and shut down their plant. Now that's really knowing your customer!

Application Challenges

- Understand the potential for working Lean projects with your customers and suppliers; but don't try it until your own house is in order and you *really* know what you're doing.

Week 52 – A Leader's Legacy (The Holidays!)

A couple of years ago I attended a retirement celebration for a longtime friend and coworker at Danfoss Power Solutions named Keith. Over the years, I've observed dozens of these celebrations. But this one was different. Speaker after speaker, some teleconferenced in from around the globe, spoke for the better part of two hours. They shared anecdotes, not so much funny or embarrassing episodes as is typically done, but stories of how Keith had personally and powerfully impacted them—their careers, their lives, their families. The tone was not so much of revelry but rather sincere gratitude.

My intent here is not to heap more praise upon Keith. There was already more of that than I'm sure he was comfortable with during his celebration (I would not have been totally surprised had he ascended directly to the heavens at its conclusion). Rather, there are some leadership lessons to be learned from Keith's example. Since that involves developing people, I think he'll be cool with this.

Keith's career at Danfoss started 40-plus years ago, on the third shift washer line. Stick an air nozzle into a hole in a cast iron part and pull the trigger. Repeat for eight hours. It doesn't get more humble than that. Even though he rose to general manager, Keith never lost that humility. He remained approachable to workers at all levels of the organization throughout his career.

Because he was humble by nature, he understood that his role was to serve those working for him so that they could do a better job making products and taking care of customers...in short, building the business. His employees weren't distracted by requests for special reports or dog and pony shows that would make him look good in the eyes of his superiors.

Keith's ability to serve others was perhaps most obvious during the tough times. During the crisis of the Great Recession, rapid and brutal cuts were required in order to keep the business solvent. Keith didn't waste his time complaining about the past imprudent "investments" that executives had made to overextend the company. Rather, he painstakingly provided regular updates to employees on what was going on and what it meant to them. During this awful time a friend confided in me, "Thank God we have Keith at the helm to guide us through this mess."

Because he wasn't focused on his own advancement, Keith oozed teamwork. But teamwork wasn't just promoted *within* his own team; it was expected *across* the teams of the larger organization. In short, the organization was bigger than his team.

Lest you get the impression that Keith was a pushover, let me share my favorite story from his celebration. Dave was a young leader with a big heart and gobs of potential. But occasionally he had the tendency to handle a personnel issue with the tact of a middle linebacker on third down and short yardage. See the issue... SMACK!

Following his first coaching session with Keith, Dave's wife asked him how his day at work went.

"OK, I guess. But I think Keith told me that I'm doing a crappy job."
"You *think* he told you?"
"Yeah, but I feel like the entire time he was talking to me, he was also giving me a big bear hug."

Author's note: Dave got the message!

Some leaders are all about customers. Others are all about the business. Some (especially engineers) can be totally into the products. And unfortunately, a few "leaders" put themselves at the center of the universe.

Keith focused on developing and serving his people, giving them new opportunities, and creating a place where teamwork was the norm. In the process he built an organization that will take care of customers, build great products, and produce impressive financial results long after his departure.

Application Challenges

■ How do you wish to be remembered? Are you doing the things today that will result in those memories?

Index

Page numbers followed by f and t indicate figures and tables, respectively.

About the Author

Prior to founding his own company, Rick enjoyed a 25-year career at Danfoss Power Solutions, a worldwide leader in the design, manufacture, and sale of engineered hydraulic and electronic systems and components used primarily in mobile equipment. Rick's career includes more than 22 years in leadership positions in engineering, operations, and continuous improvement.

Rick's accomplishments in engineering include leading the development of two very successful products in record time. He has served as production manager for union and non-union factories in Iowa and Illinois, with responsibility for as many as 300 employees.

His real passion, however, involves continuous improvement. While at Danfoss, he served as the Six Sigma Master Black Belt for the company's North American plants and was the lead Lean practitioner for the North American Propel division. While in the latter position, he guided a multimillion-dollar value stream to world class metrics of 100 percent on-time delivery, 280 defects per million at the customer's assembly line (99.972 percent good), and 35 inventory turns.

Throughout his career, Rick has been recognized as a people developer, hiring and growing leaders now located around the globe. He has created and delivered several training courses, and thoroughly enjoys helping adults learn and apply new knowledge. His blue-collar upbringing allows him to relate to hourly employees as well as senior leaders. He has coached the senior leaders of several organizations ranging in size from $2 million to $200 million.

Janet and Rick have been married since 1982. They have three married children and five (soon to be seven) grandchildren.

Rick enjoys reading and playing guitar as well at outdoor activities such as biking, hiking, cross country skiing, and fishing.

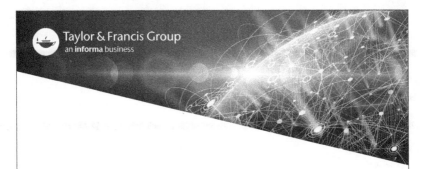